I0714455

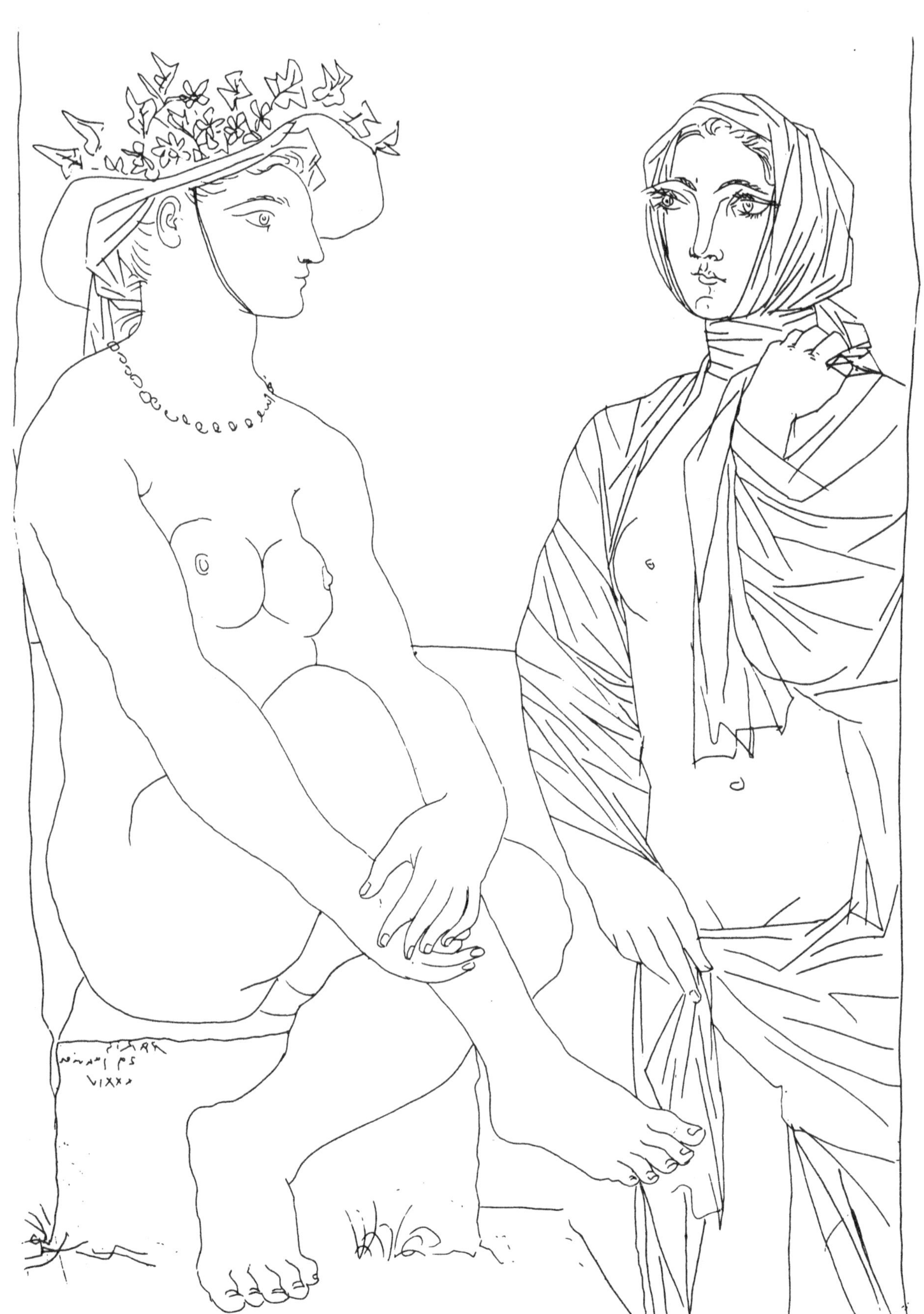

PICASSO
LINE DRAWINGS AND PRINTS

44 Works by Pablo Picasso

Dover Publications, Garden City, New York

Pablo Picasso (1881–1973) is undoubtedly the towering figure of twentieth-century art. An indefatigable artist whose career began in childhood and continued throughout his life, he is perhaps best known for his paintings, which pioneered or reflected many major trends. But the exercise of his powers in other media was no less prolific. The fecundity of his imagination and brilliance of his technique are nowhere better displayed than in his line drawings and prints.

Of the works presented here, the best-known are those in Picasso's neoclassical style, which he began to develop during a trip through Italy in 1917. Executed in contour, they reveal the artist's profound sensitivity of line and thorough understanding of human anatomy. Combining the two, he is able to create poses with a breathtaking inventive freedom that only a few artists, such as Titian, have possessed.

Many of the works on these pages, such as the illustrations for Balzac's *Le Chef-d'oeuvre inconnu*, were executed for the legendary art dealer Ambroise Vollard. In his *Recollections of a Picture Dealer,* Vollard said of them: ". . . Cubist realisations rub shoulders with drawings that remind one of Ingres [*see page 23*]. But each new work of Picasso's shocks the public, till the day when astonishment gives way to admiration."

Copyright

Copyright © 1981 by Dover Publications
All rights reserved.

Bibliographical Note

Picasso Line Drawings and Prints is a new work,
first published by Dover Publication in 1981.

International Standard Book Number

ISBN-13: 978-0-486-24196-8
ISBN-10: 0-486-24196-3

Printed in Canada
24196326   2025
www.doverpublications.com

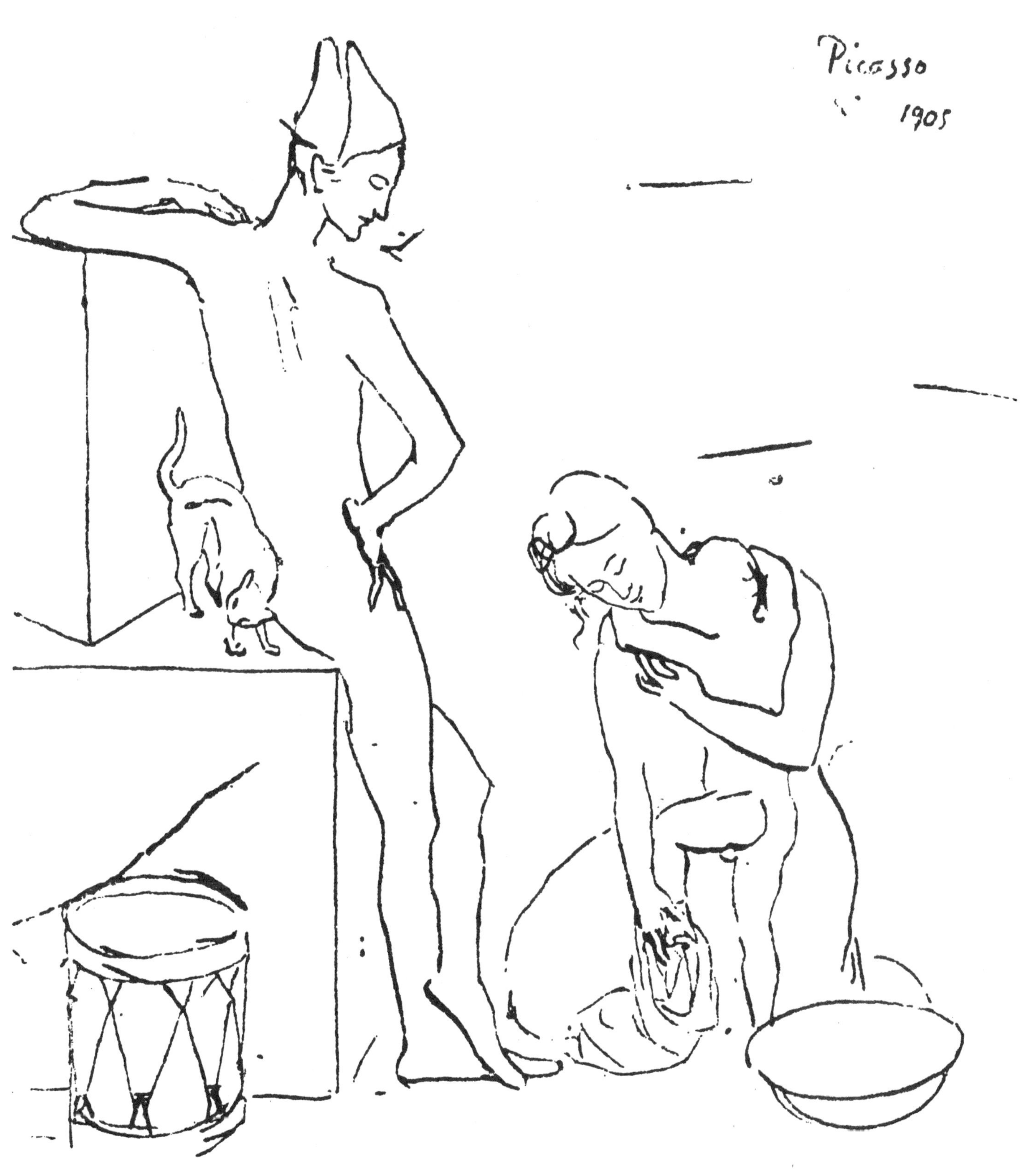

THE BATH. 1905. Drypoint. 34.4 x 28.9 cm (13⁹⁄₁₆ x 11⅜ inches).   1

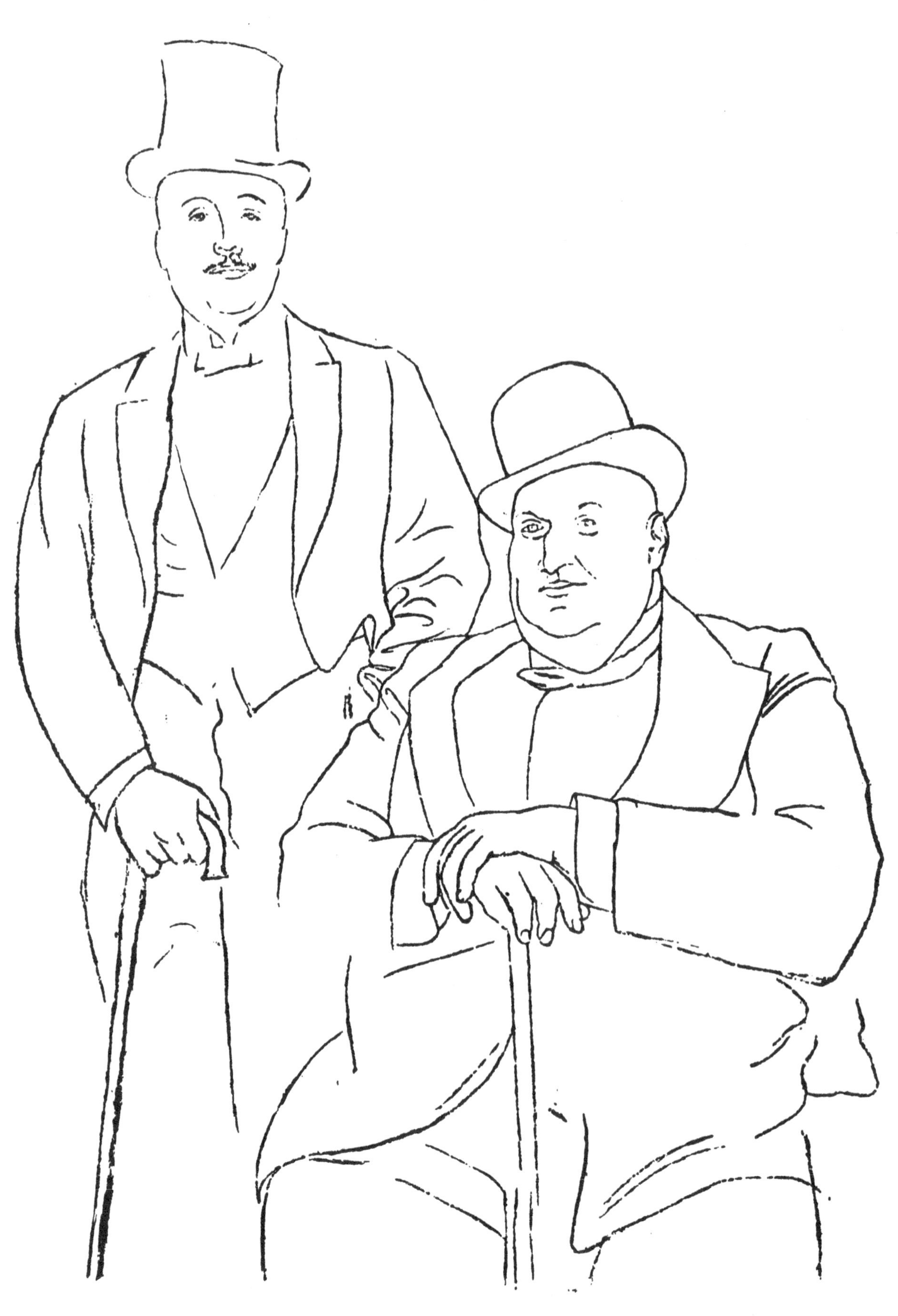

SERGE DIAGHILEV AND ALFRED SELIGSBERG. 1919. Charcoal and pencil. 63.5 x 49.6 cm (25 x 19⅛ inches).

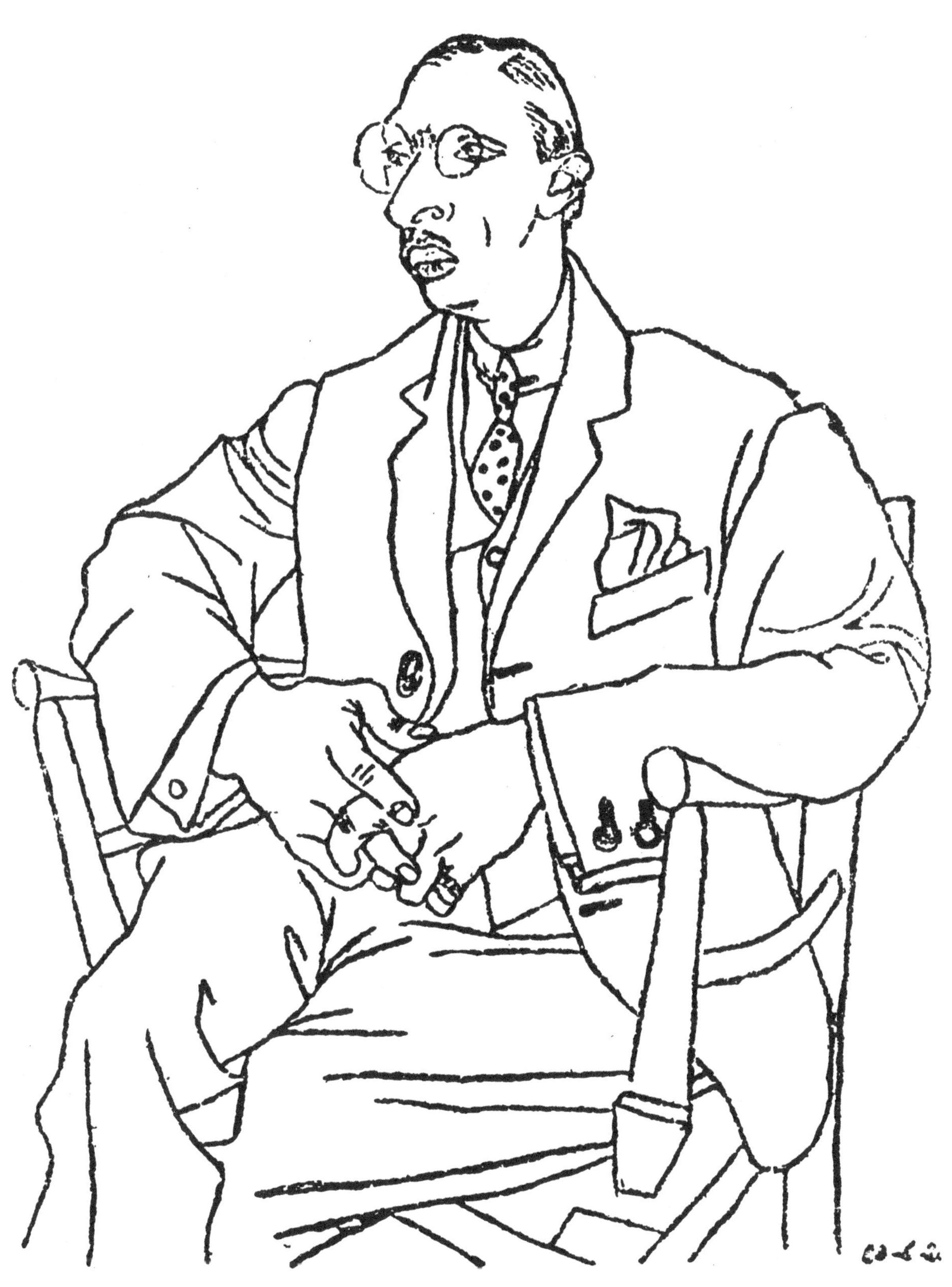

Igor Stravinsky. 1920. Pencil. 62 x 48.5 cm (24⅜ x 19⅛ inches).

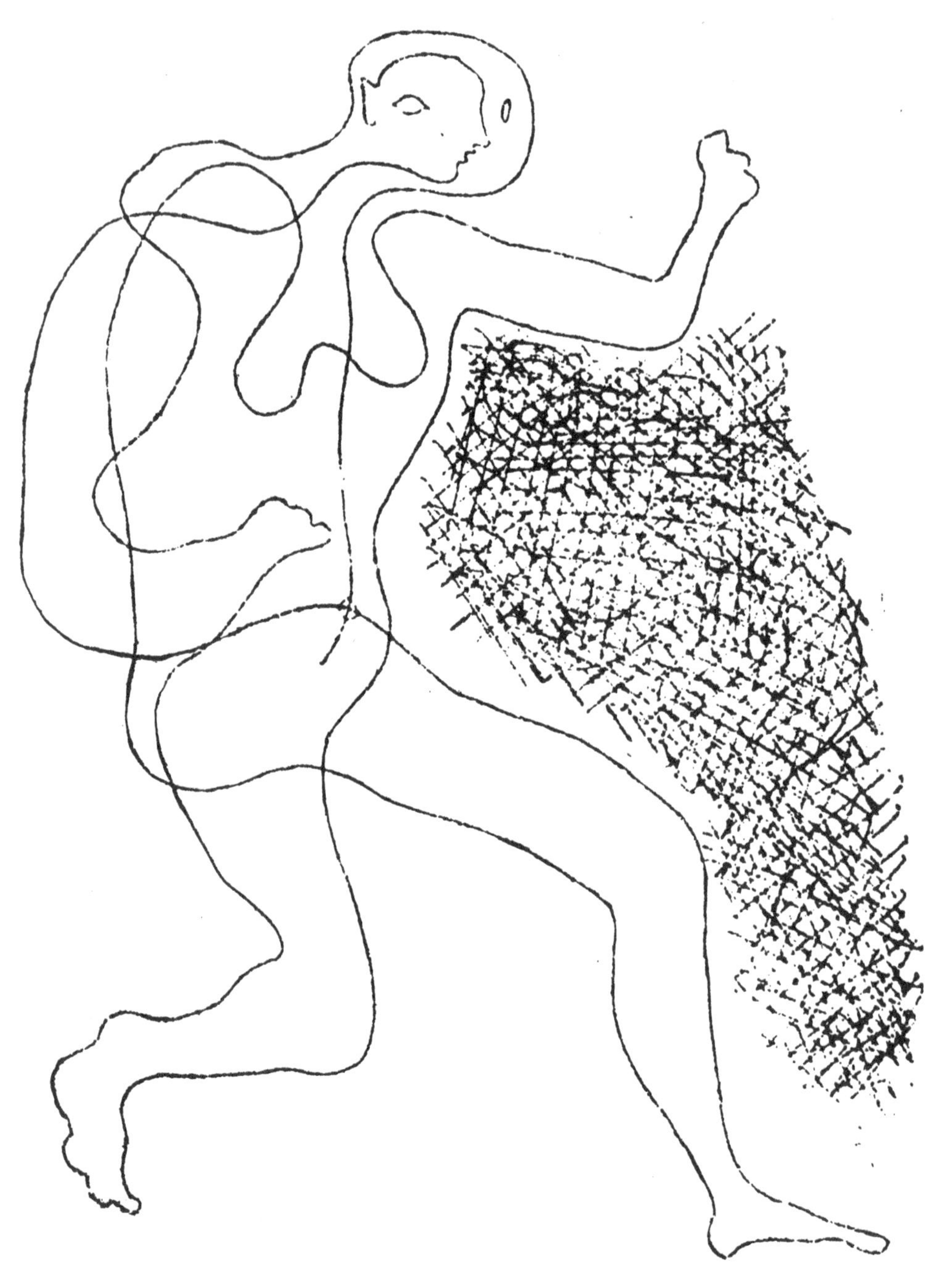

Figure Study.

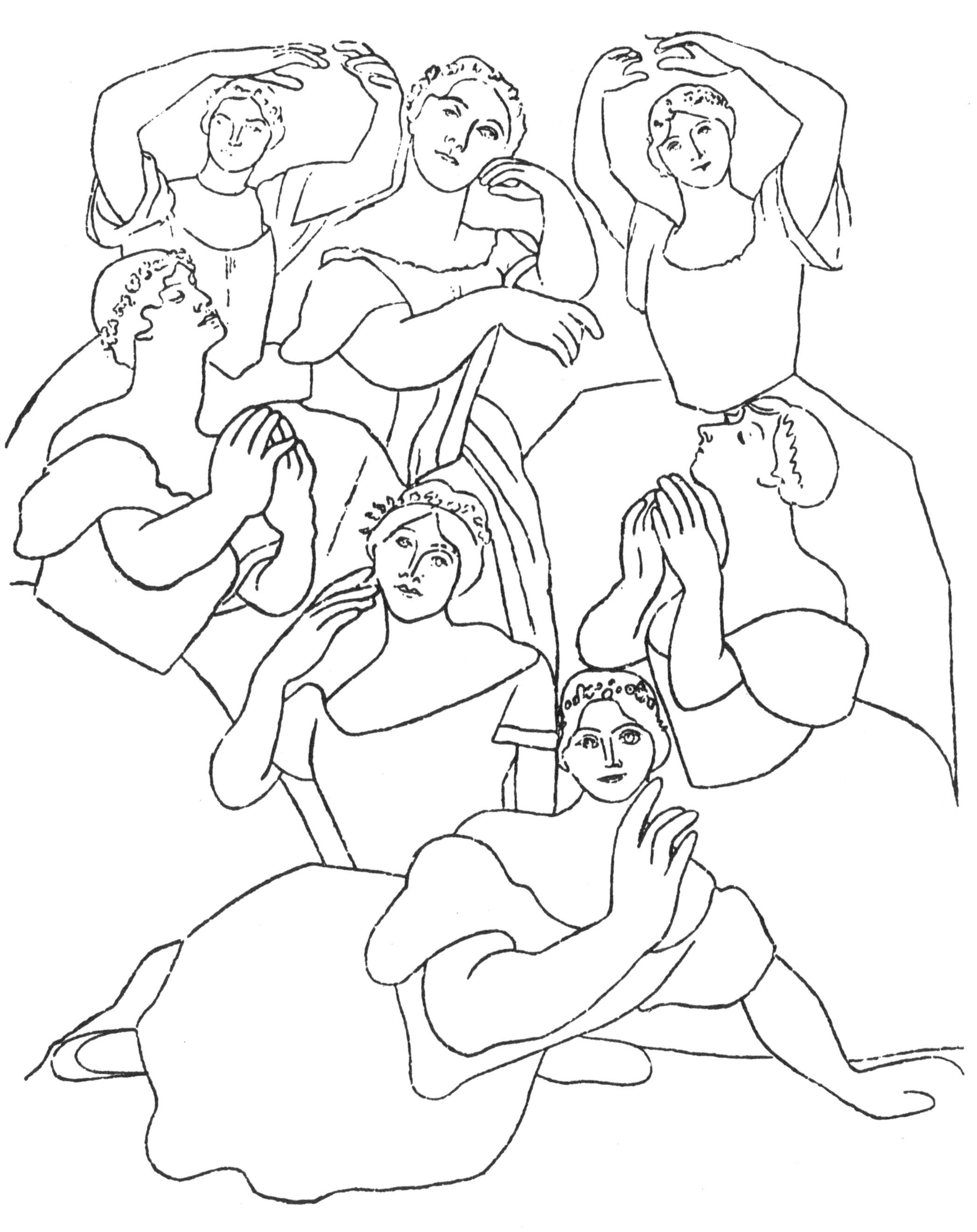

Seven Dancers. 1919. Pencil. 62.2 x 50 cm (24½ x 19¾ inches).

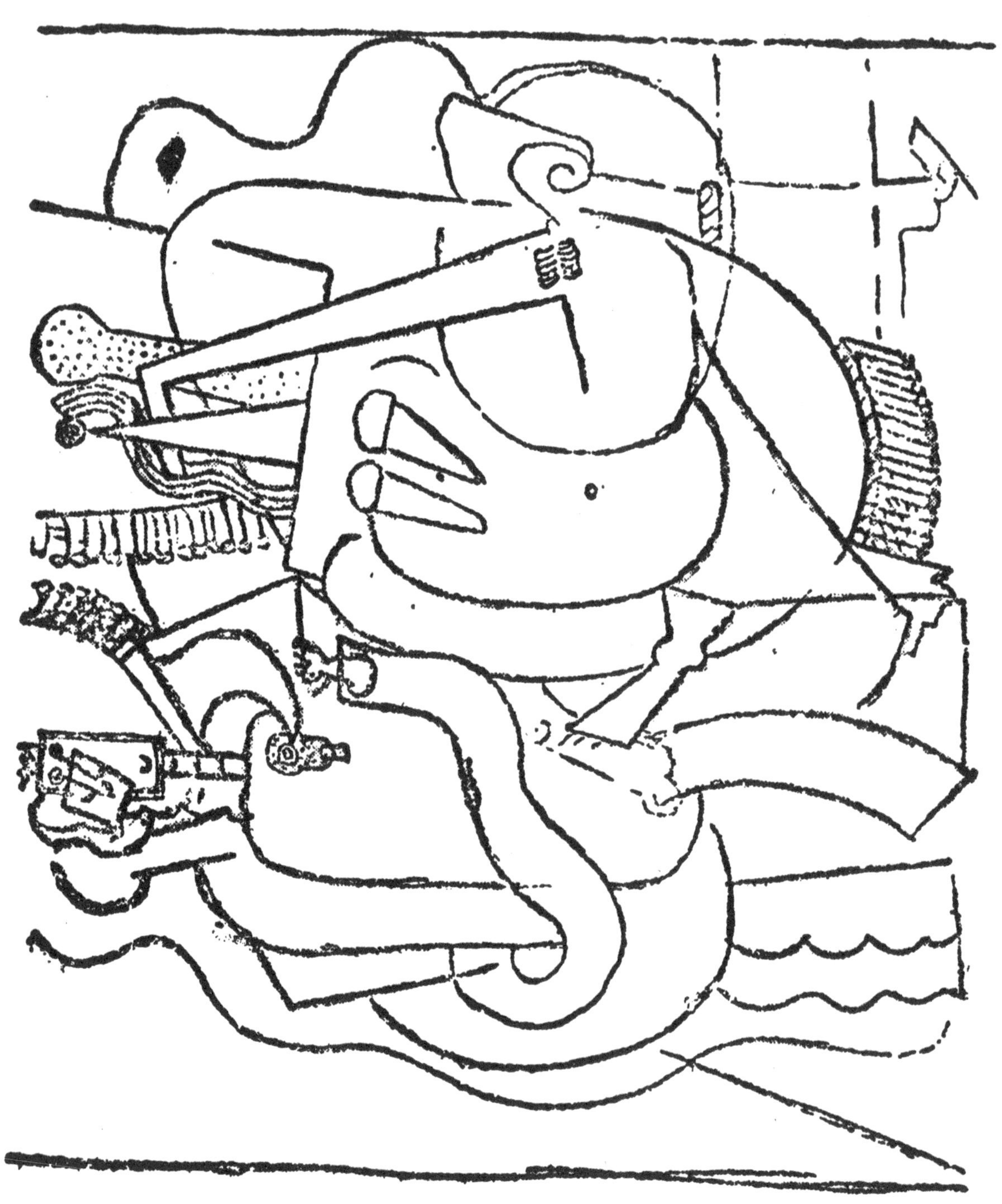

Cubist Study.

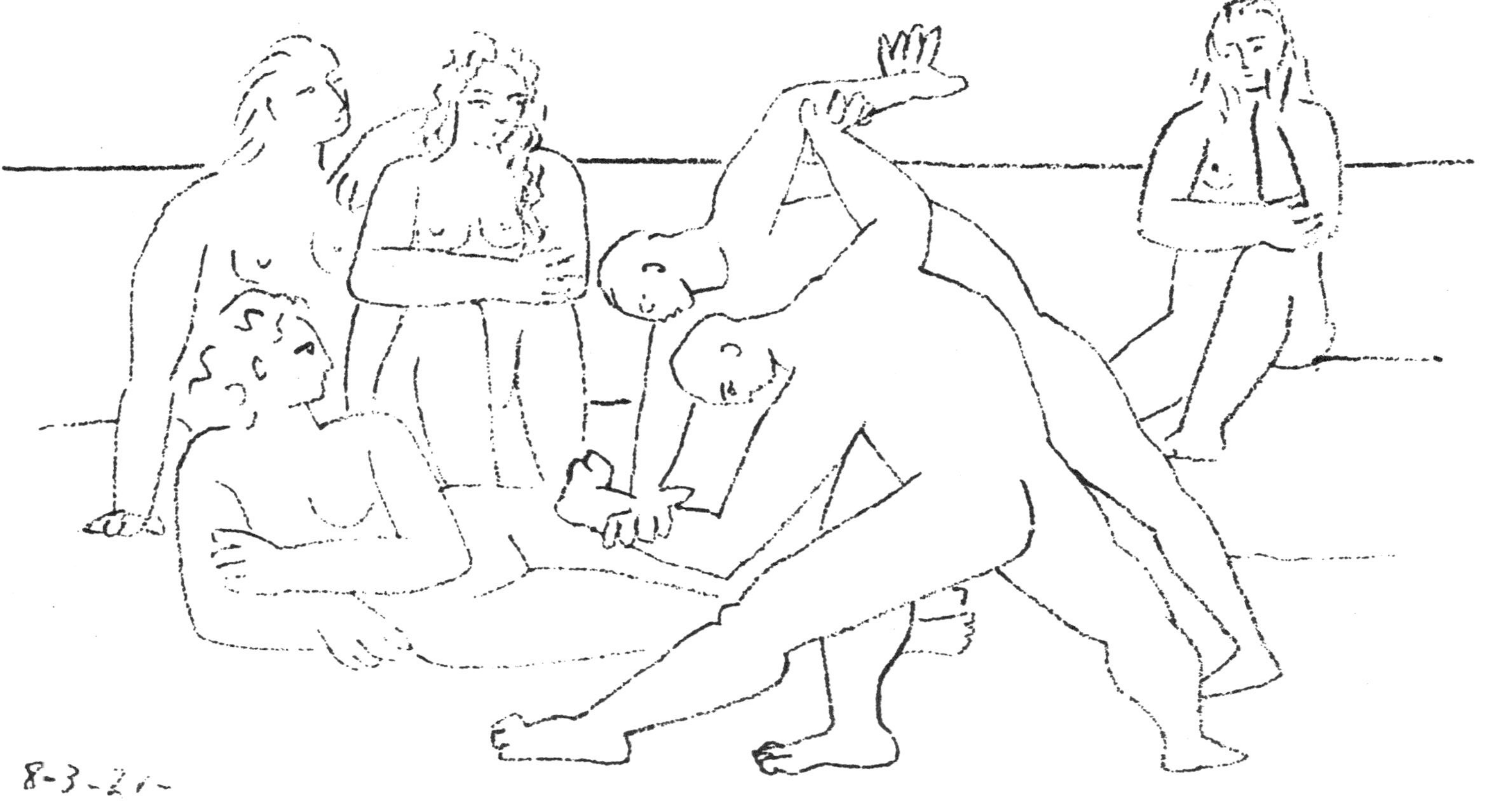

MEN WRESTLING. From *Quatre Lithographies.* 1921. Lithograph. 10 x 22 cm ($3^{15}/_{16}$ x $8^{11}/_{16}$ inches.)

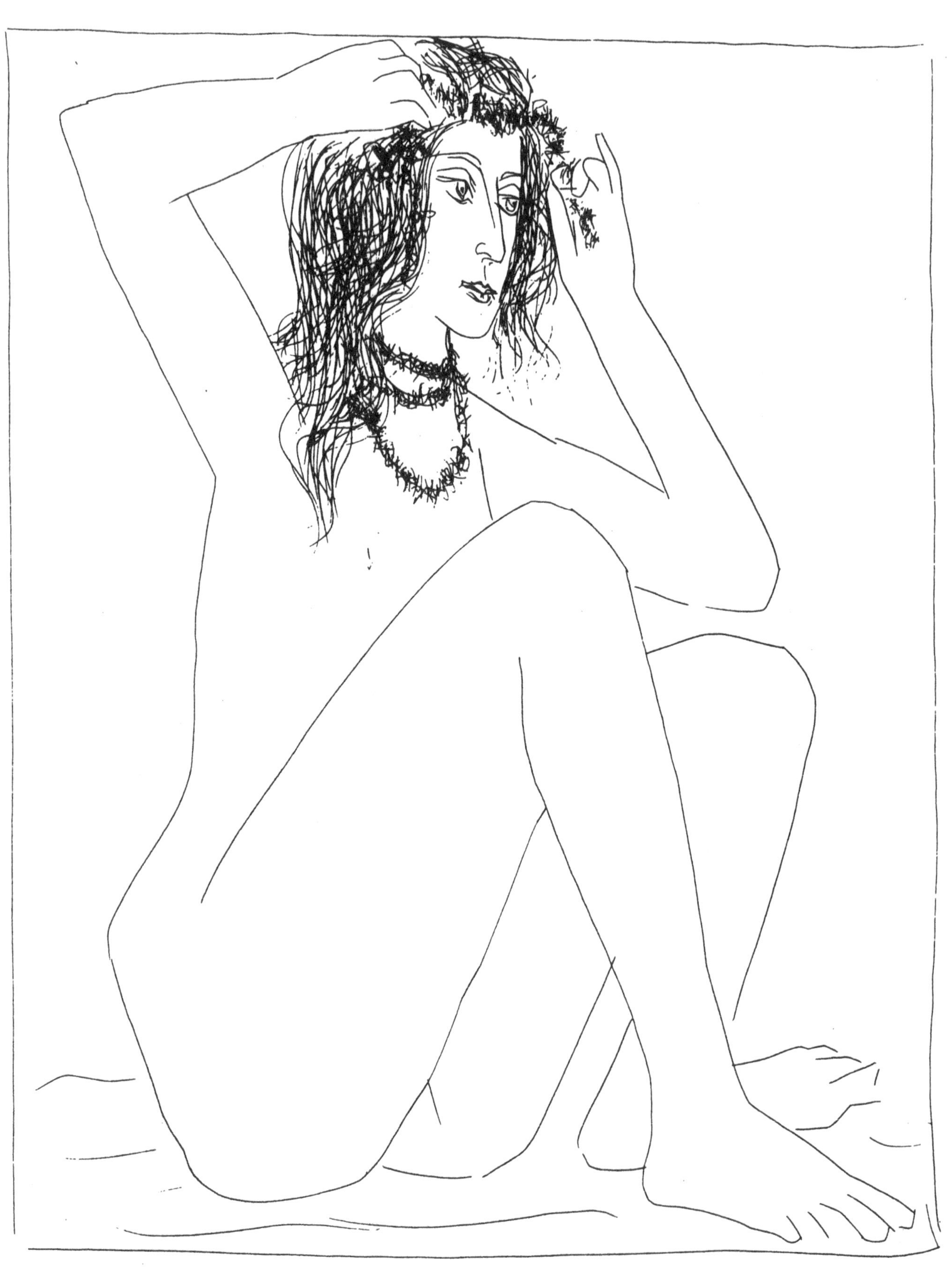

SEATED NUDE CROWNING HERSELF WITH FLOWERS. 1930. Etching. 30.9 x 22.2 cm (12⅜
x 8¾ inches).

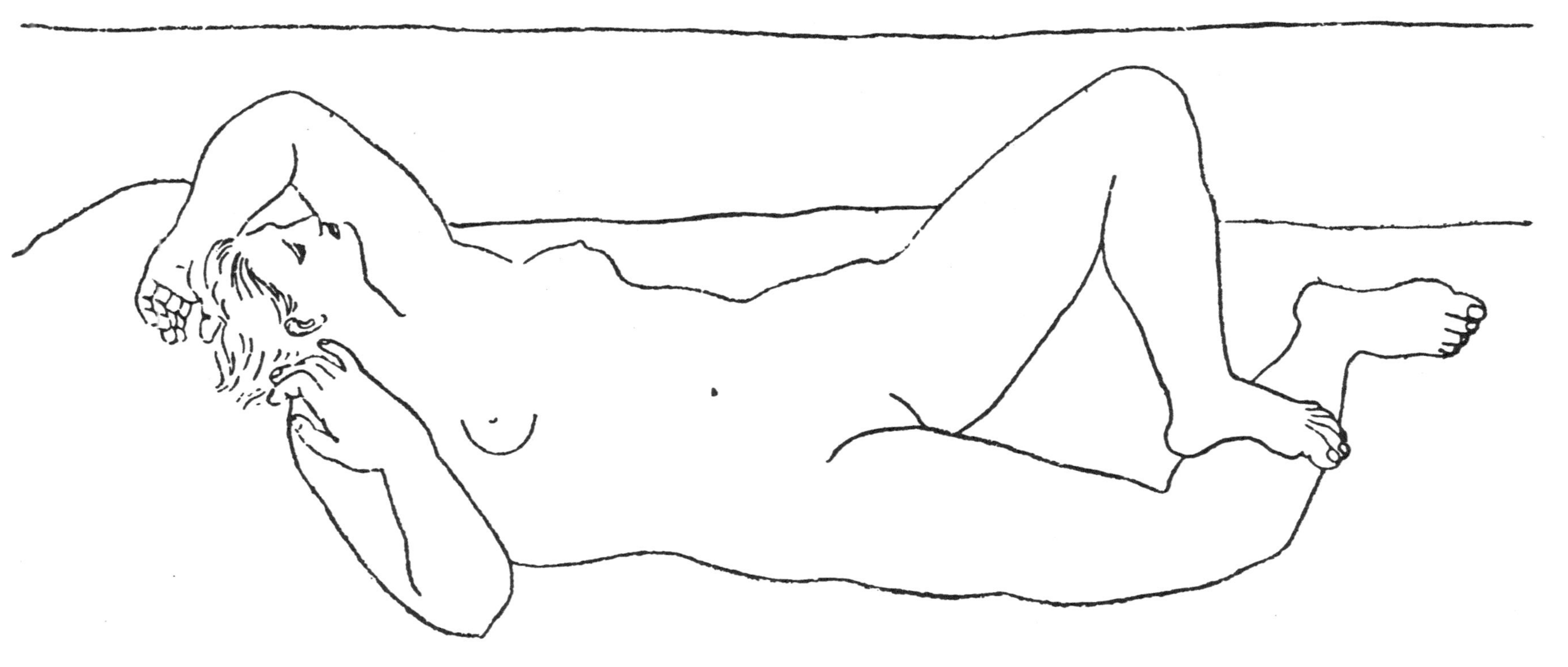

Reclining Nude. 1920. Lead pencil. 48 x 63 cm (18⅞ x 23¾ inches).

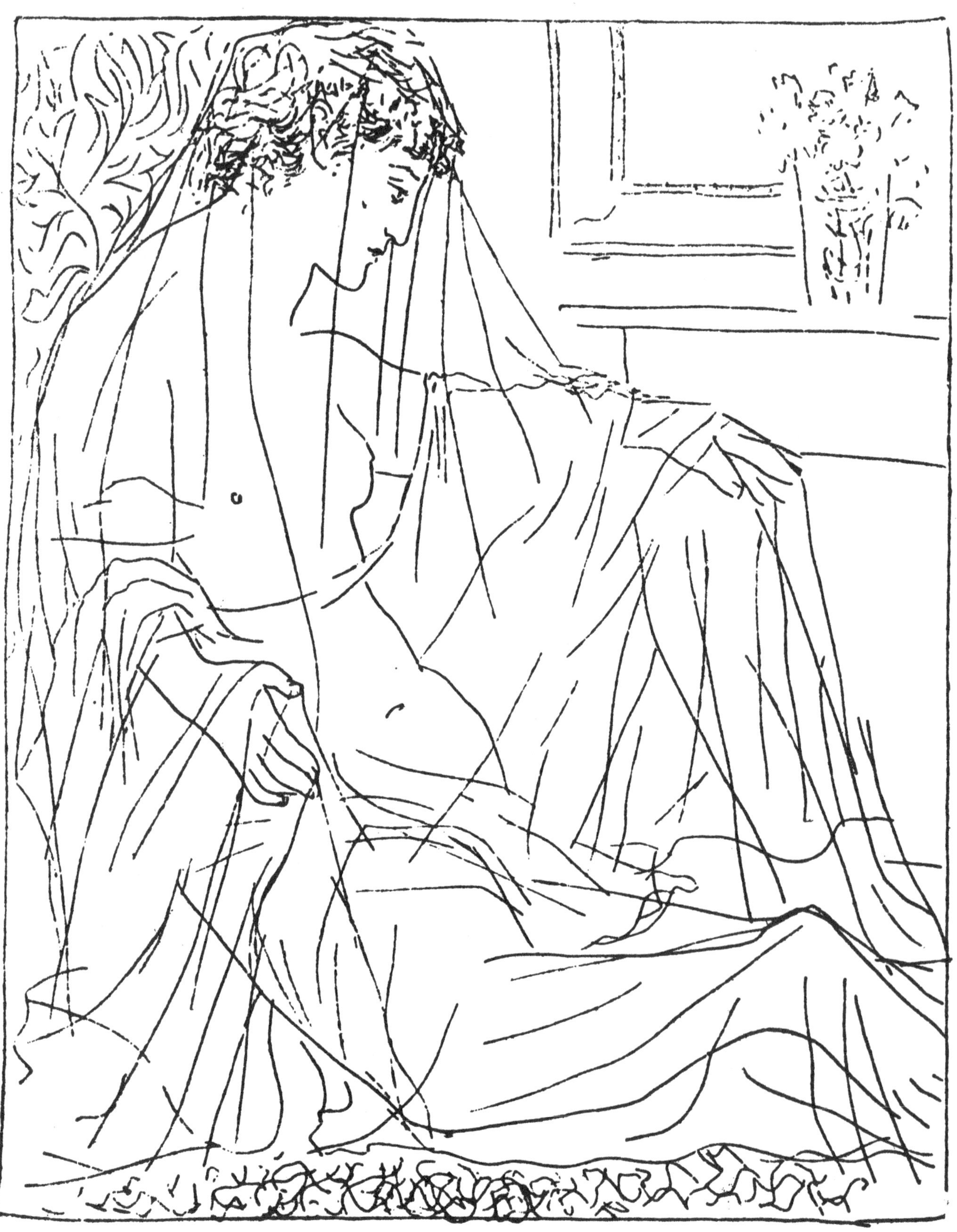

DRAPED FIGURE.

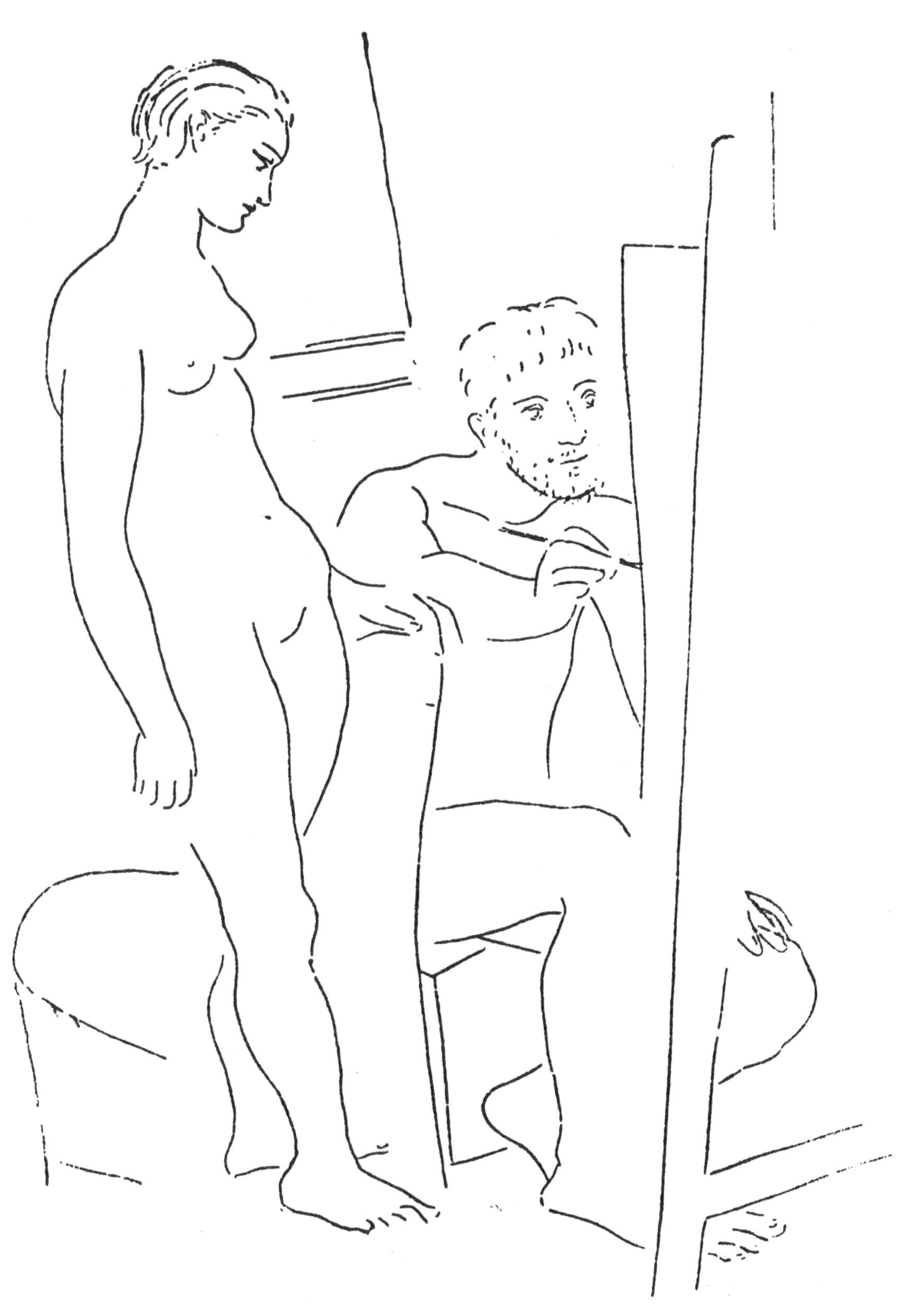

MODEL AND PAINTER.

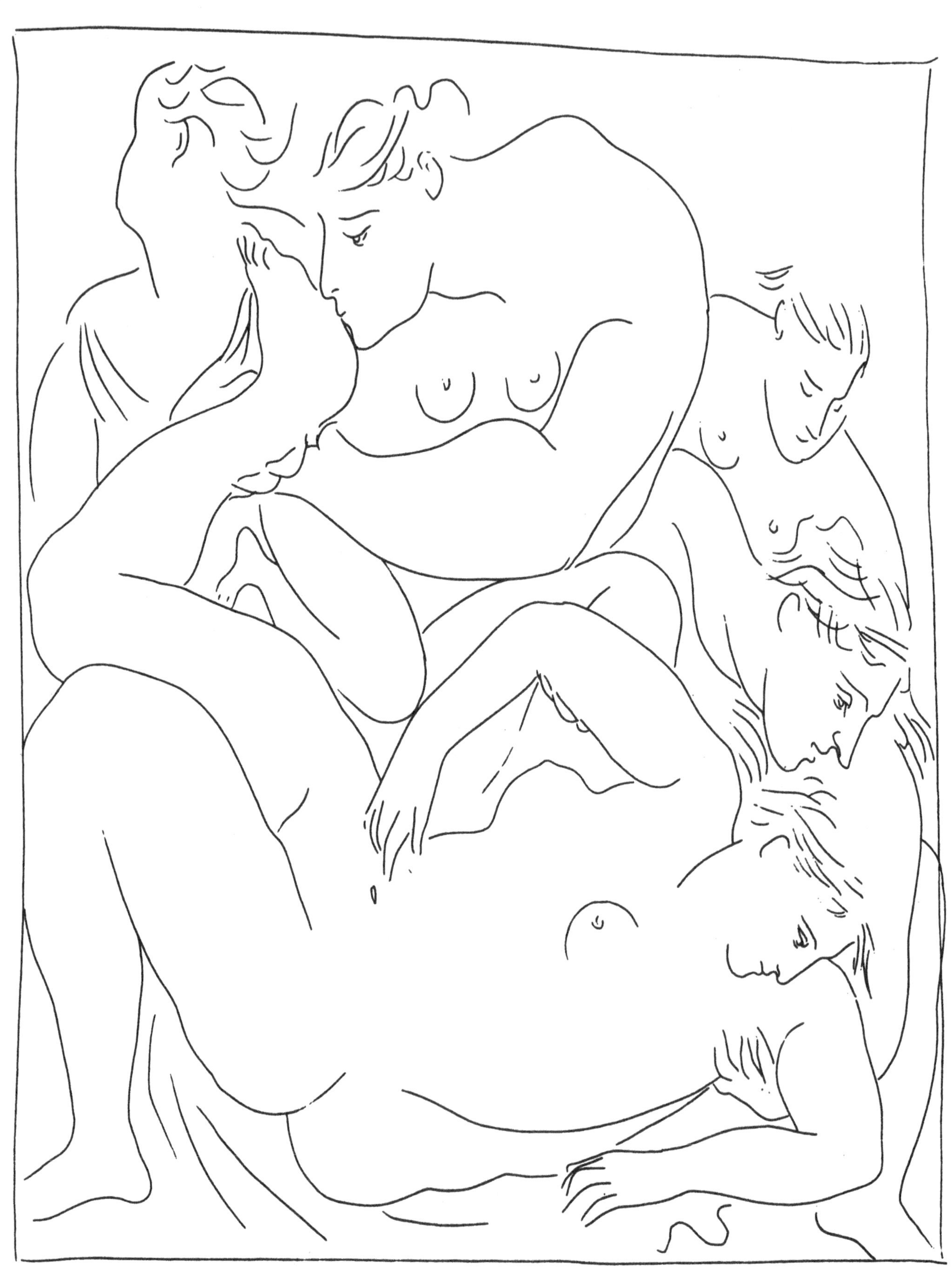

EURYDICE STUNG BY A SERPENT. From *Les Métamorphoses* (1931). 1930. Etching. 22.3 x 17 cm ($8^{13}/_{16}$ x $6^{11}/_{16}$ inches).

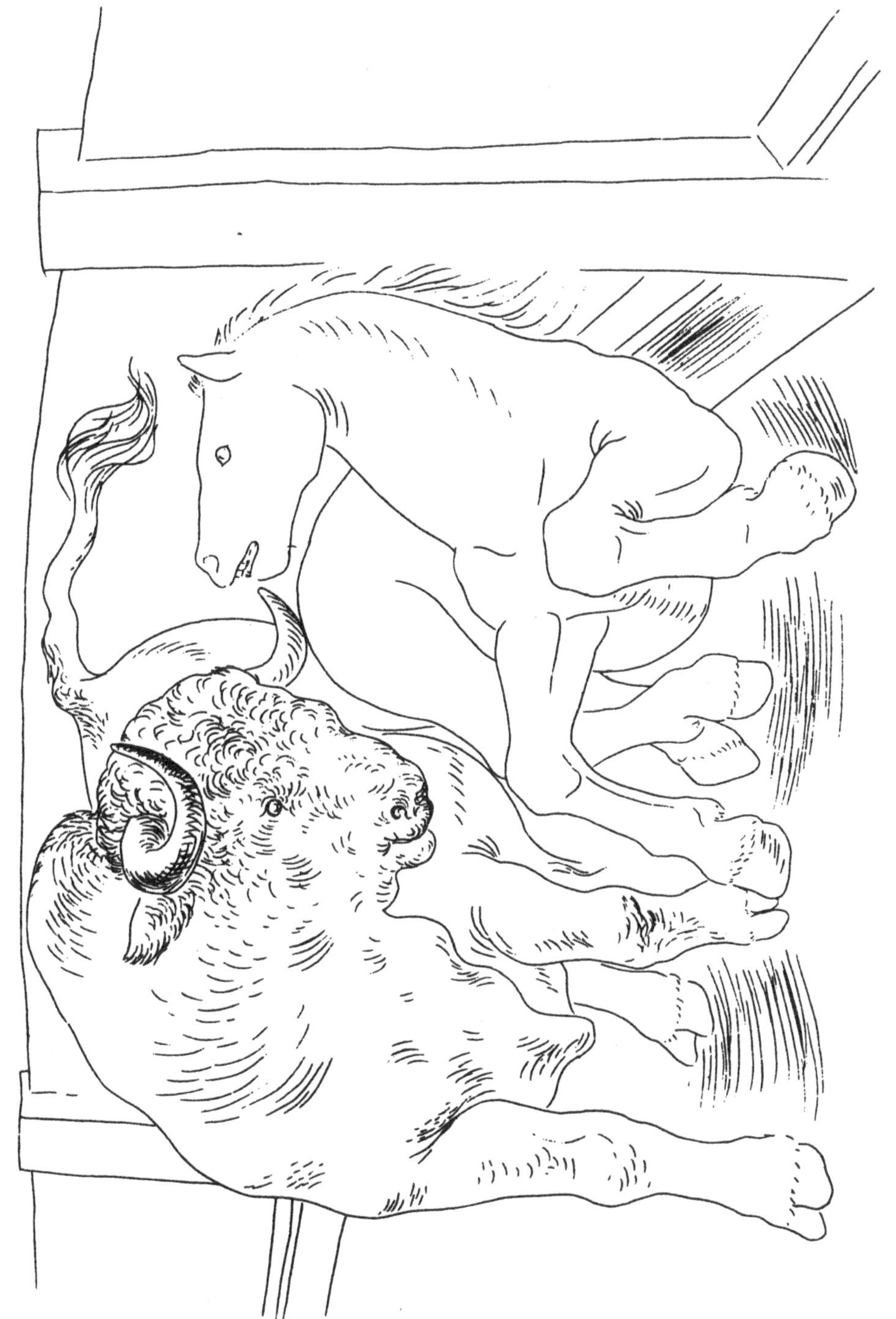

BULL AND HORSE. From *Le Chef-d'oeuvre inconnu* (1931). 1927. Etching. 19.2 x 27.9 cm (7⁹⁄₁₆ x 11 inches).

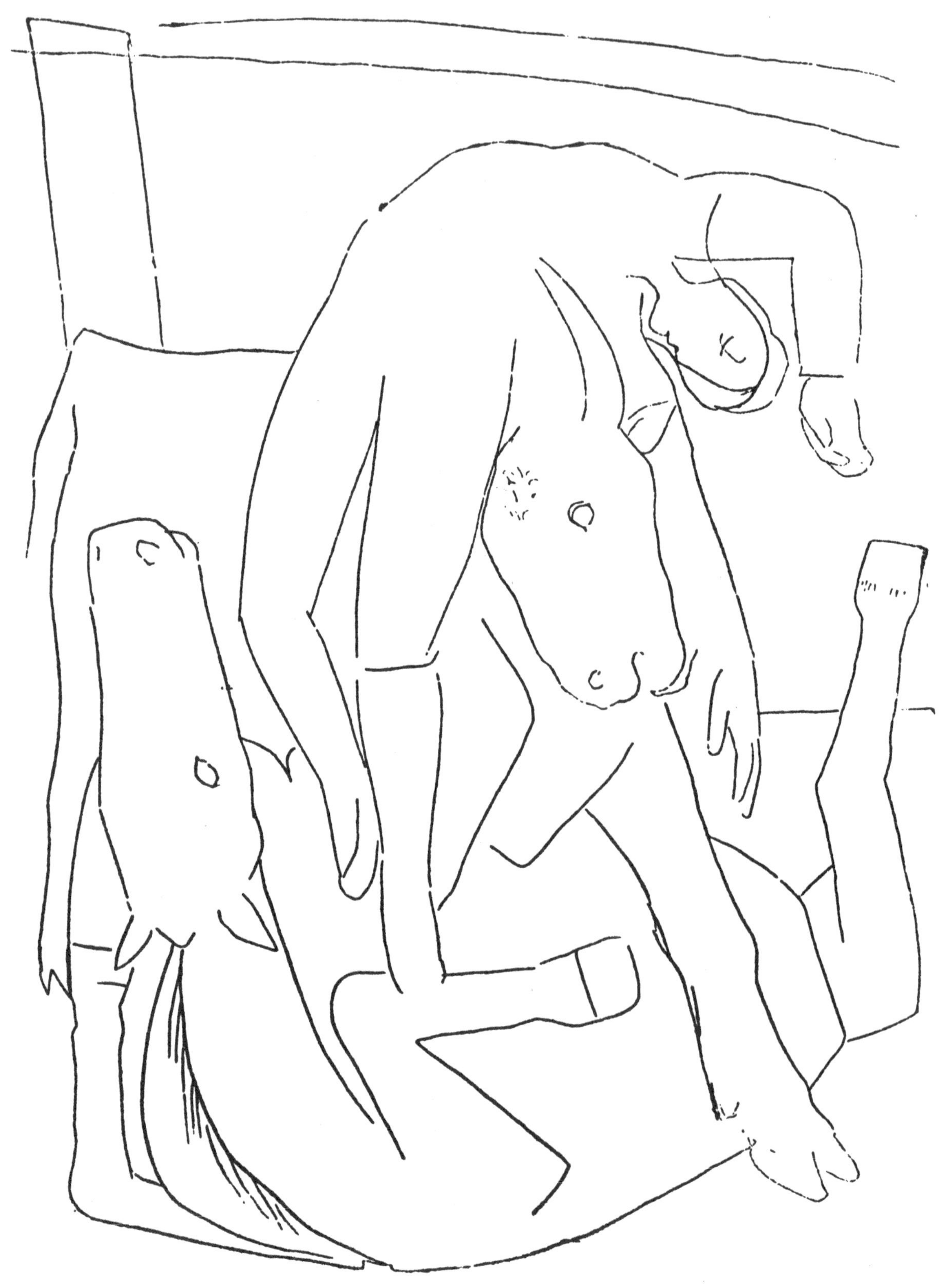

                    GORED MATADOR.

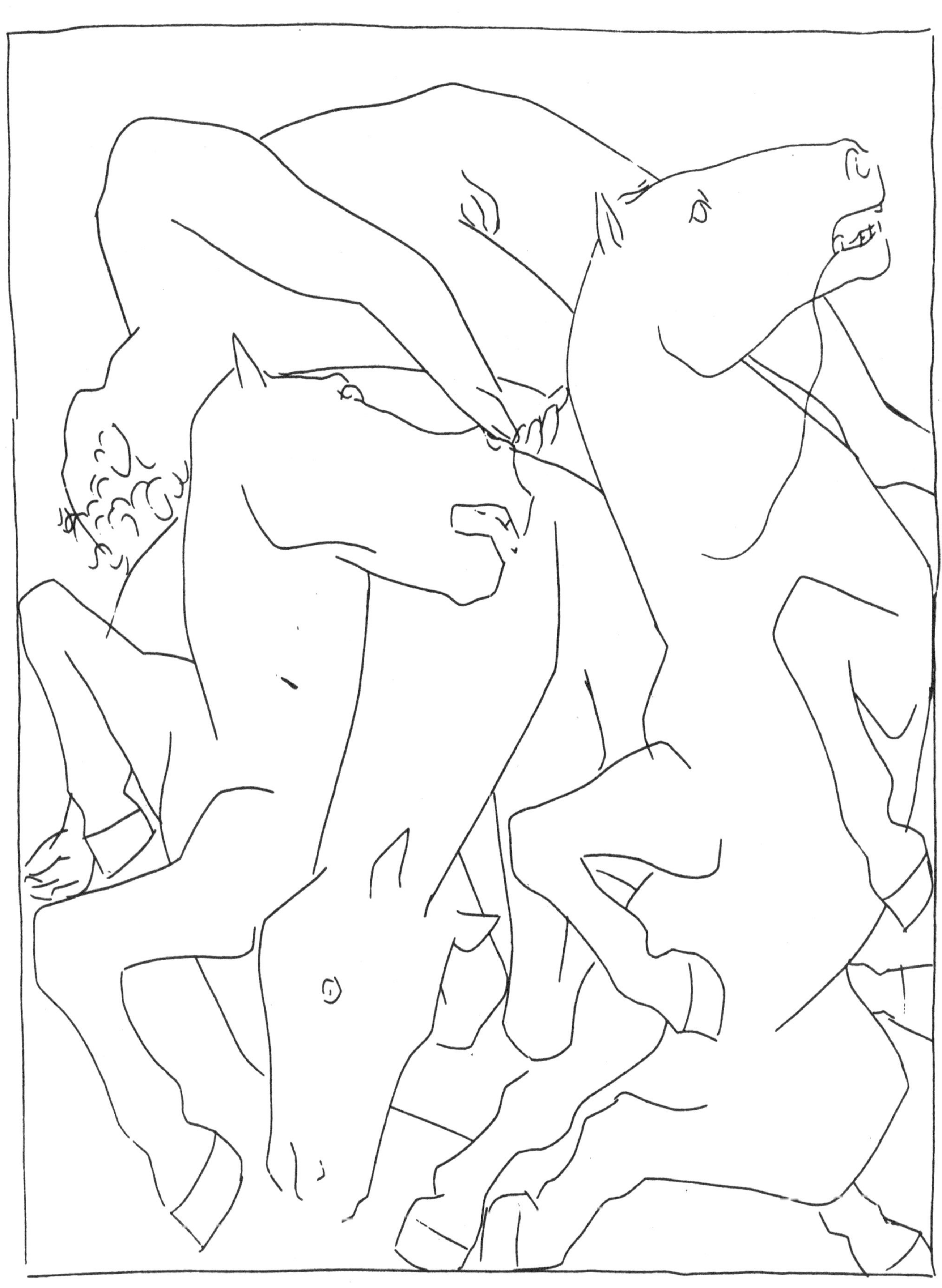

The Fall of Phaethon with the Chariot of the Sun. From Les Métamorphoses
(1931). 1930. Etching. 22.3 x 17 cm (8¹³/₁₆ x 6¹¹/₁₆ inches).   15

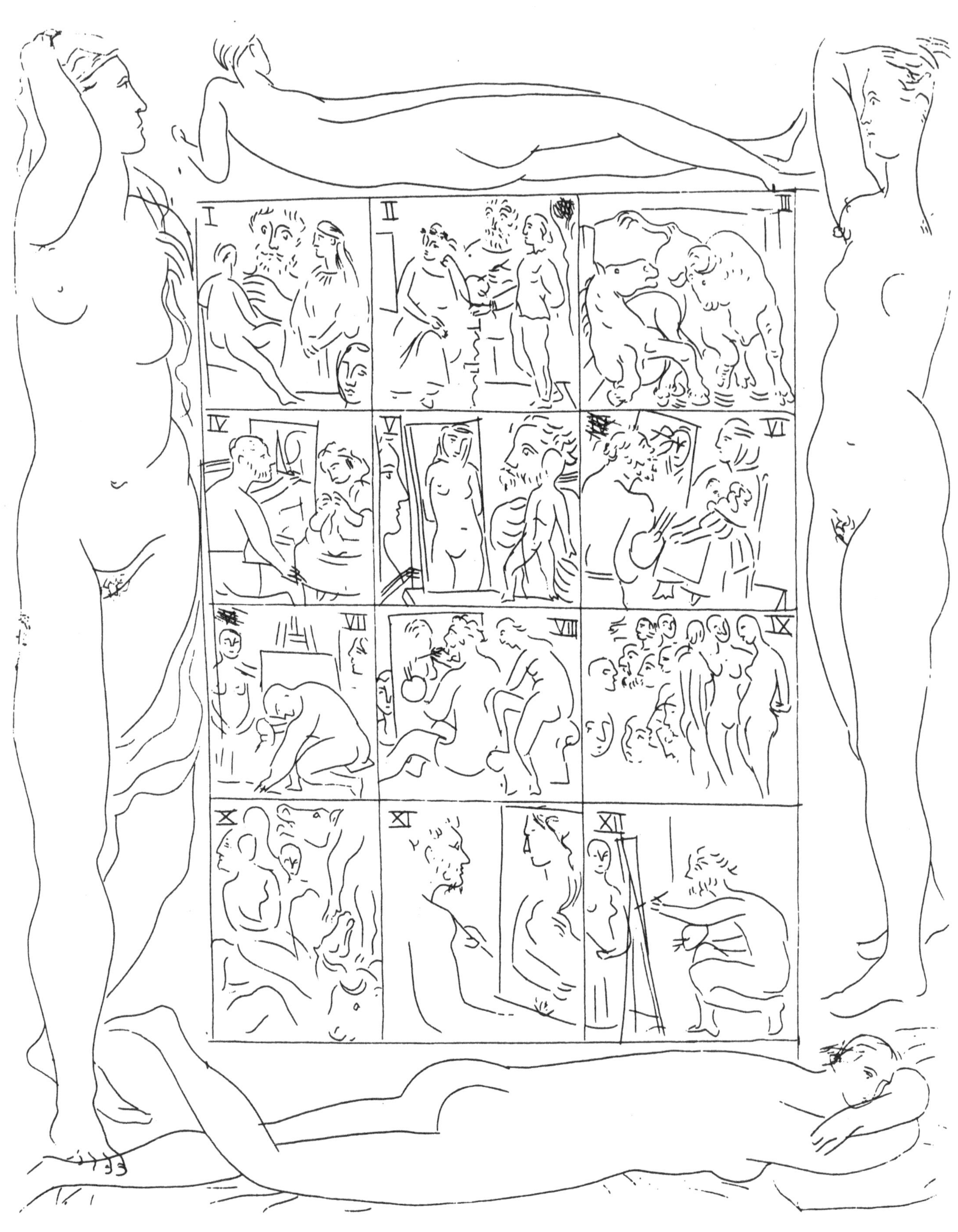

TABLE OF ETCHINGS. From *Le Chef-d'oeuvre inconnu* (1931). 1931. Etching. 37.5 x 29.8 cm (14¾ x 11¾ inches).

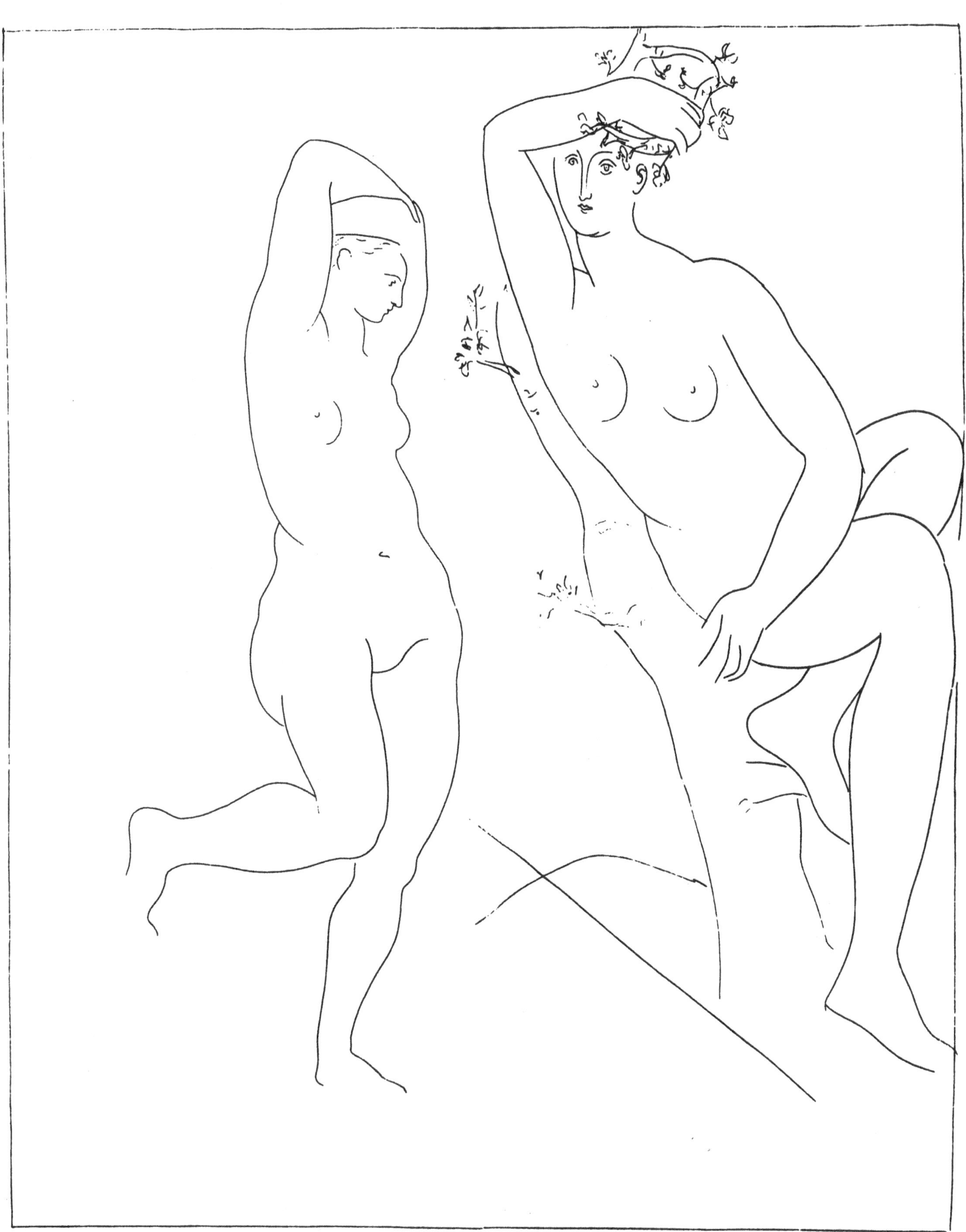

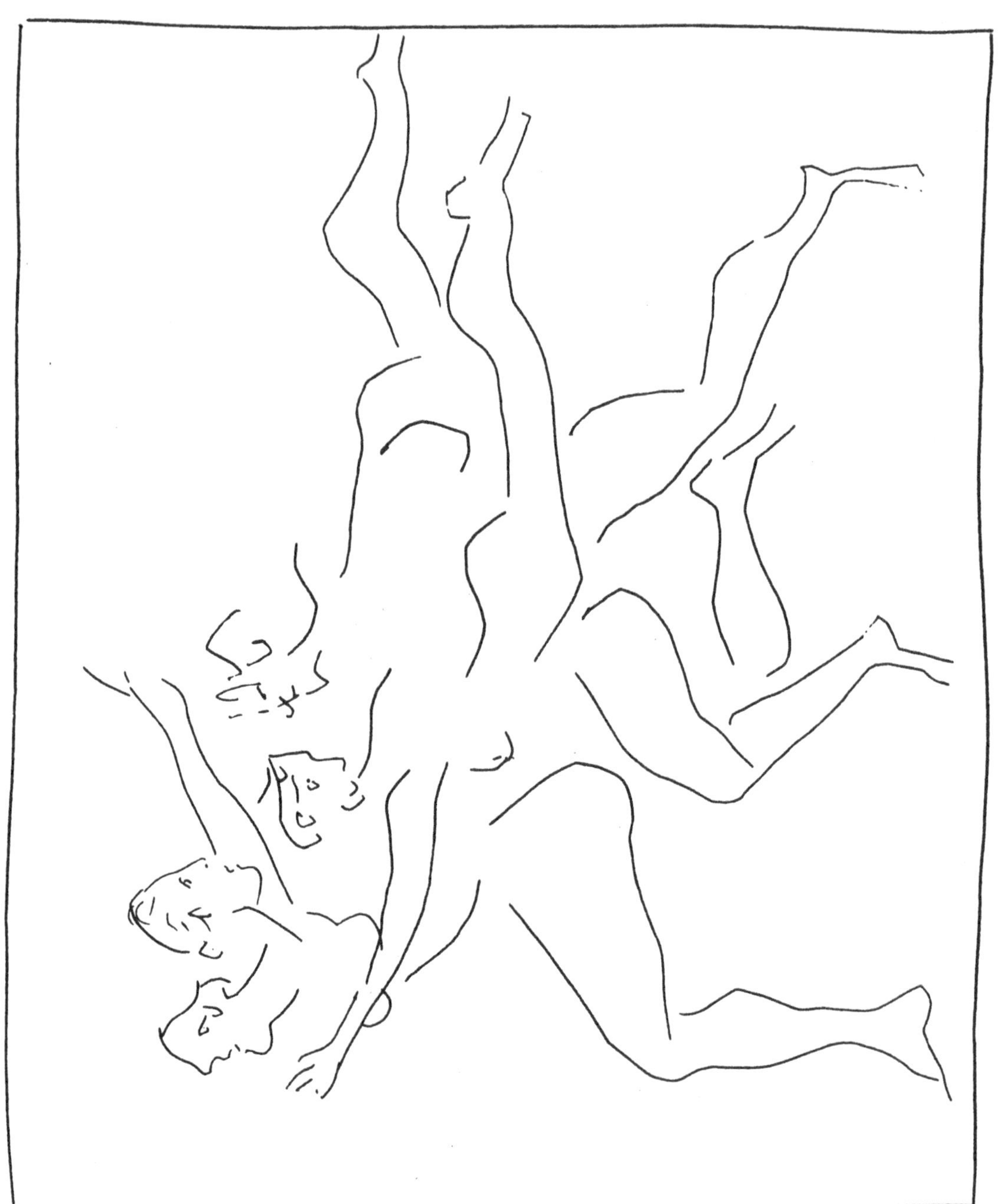

Four Women in Flight. From *Les Métamorphoses* (1931). 1931. Etching. 13.6 x 17.1 cm (5³⁄₈ x 16³⁄₄ inches).

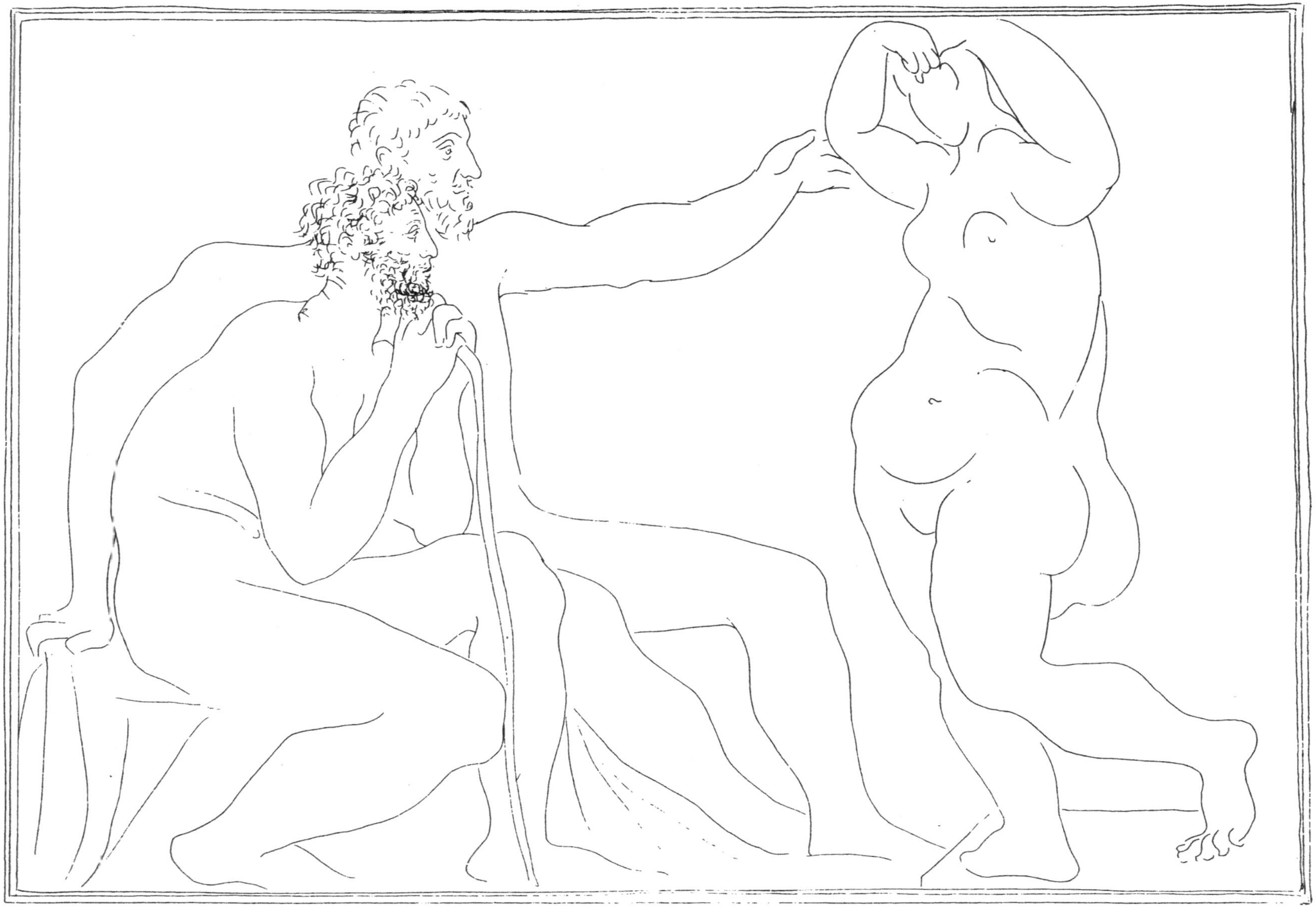

Two Sculptors Before a Statue. 1931. Etching. 22.2 x 32 cm (8¾ x 12⁵⁄₁₆ inches).

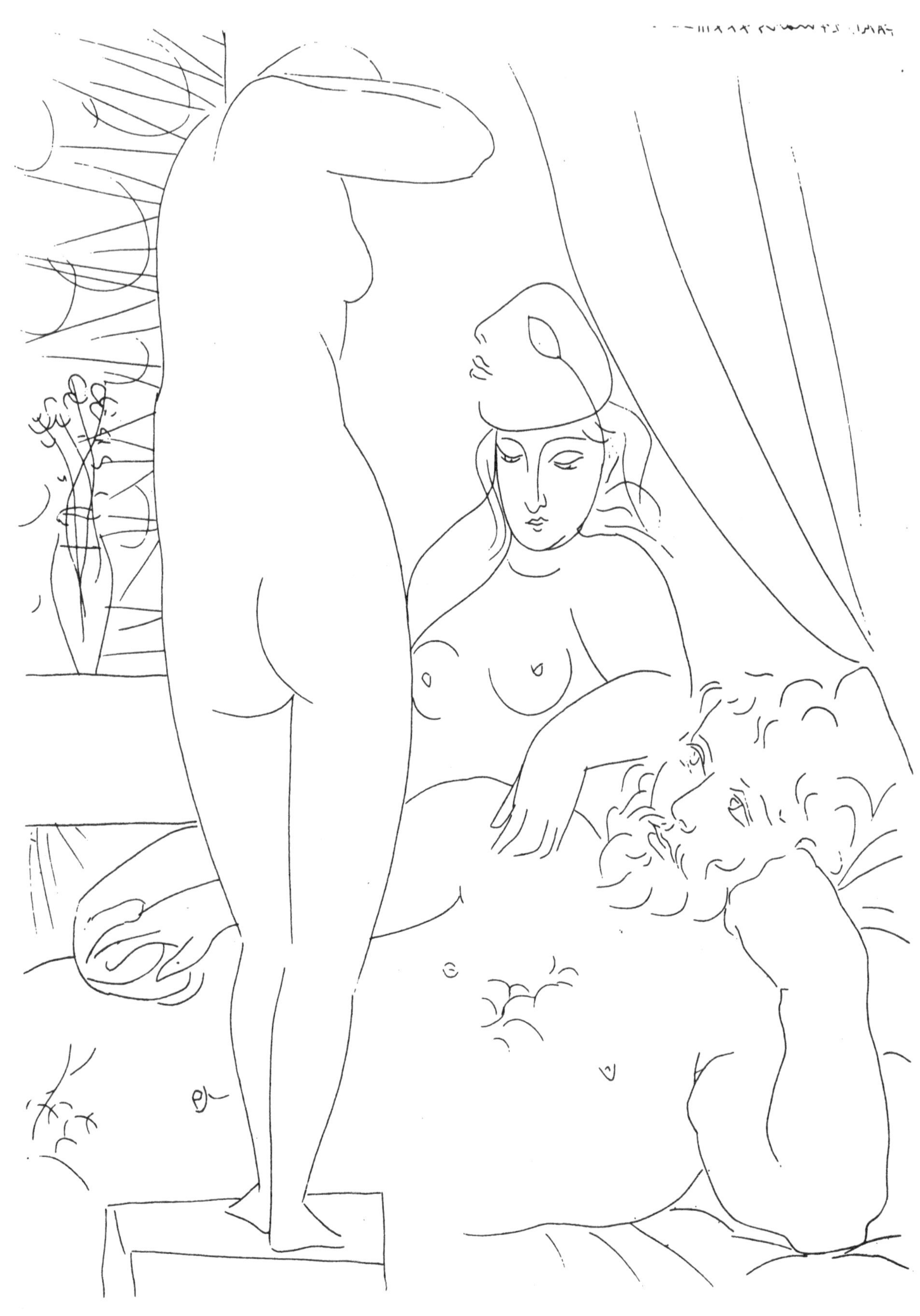

Model, Sculptor and Statue. 1933. Etching. 26.8 x 19.4 cm (10½ x 7⅝ inches).

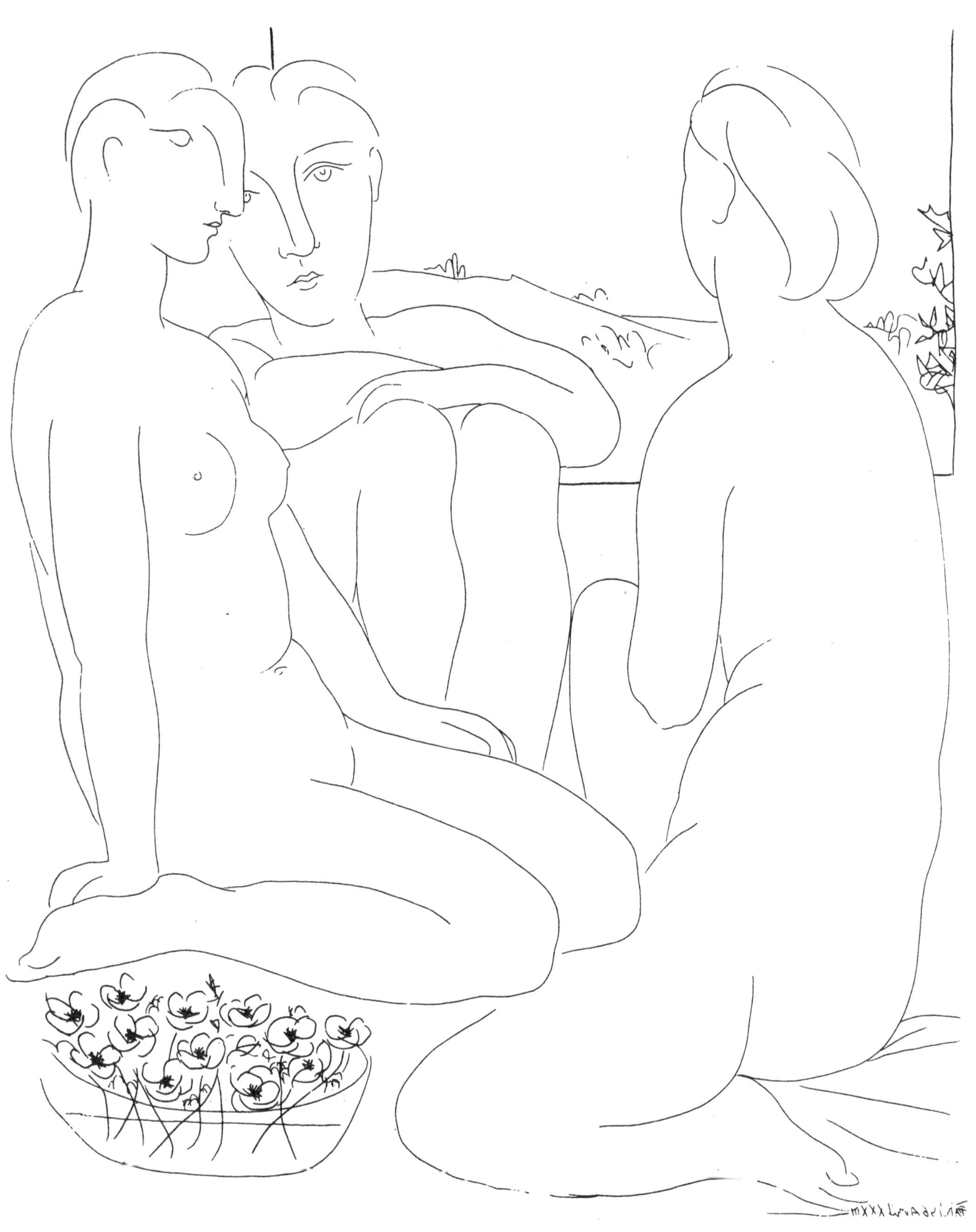

Three Seated Nudes. 1933. Etching. 37.7 x 29. 8 cm ($14\frac{7}{16}$ x $11\frac{3}{4}$ inches).

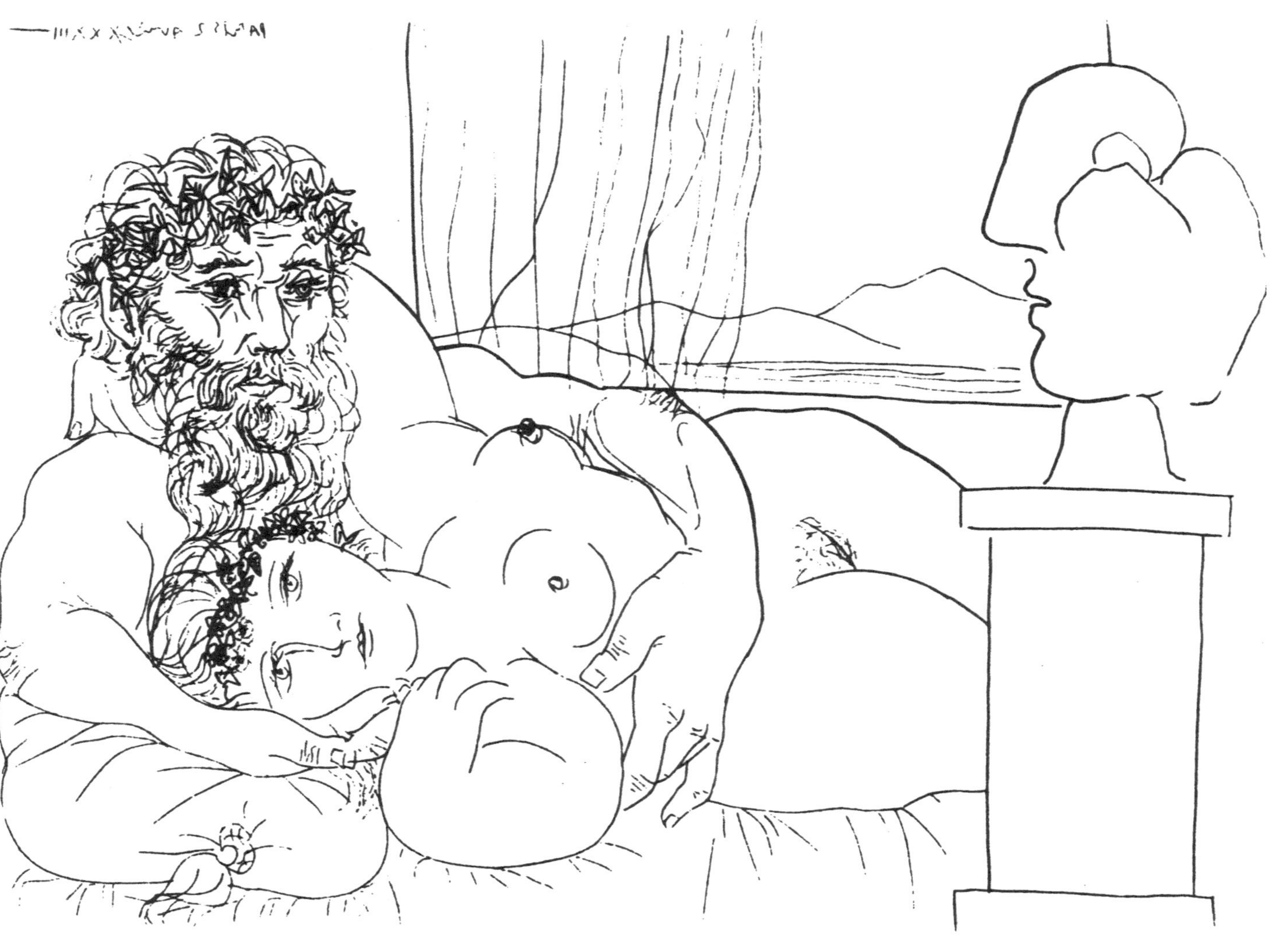

Sculptor at Rest, Holding the Model in His Arms and Looking at a Sculptured Head. 1933: 19.3 x 26.7 cm (7⅝ x 10½ inches).

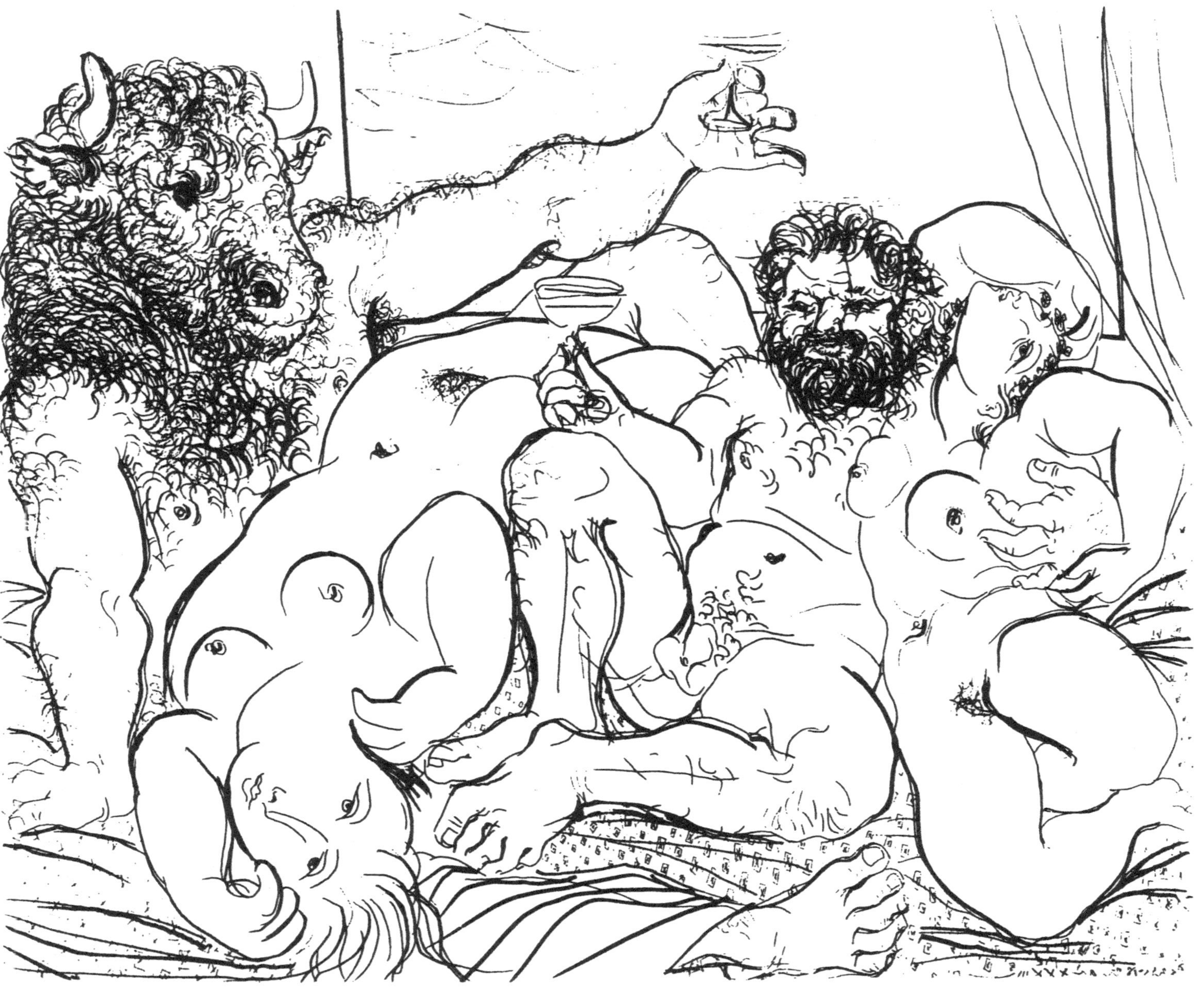

Minotaur Drinking with Sculptor and Two Girls. 1933. Combined technique.
29.7 x 36.6 cm (11^{11}/$_{16}$ x 14^{3}/$_{8}$ inches).

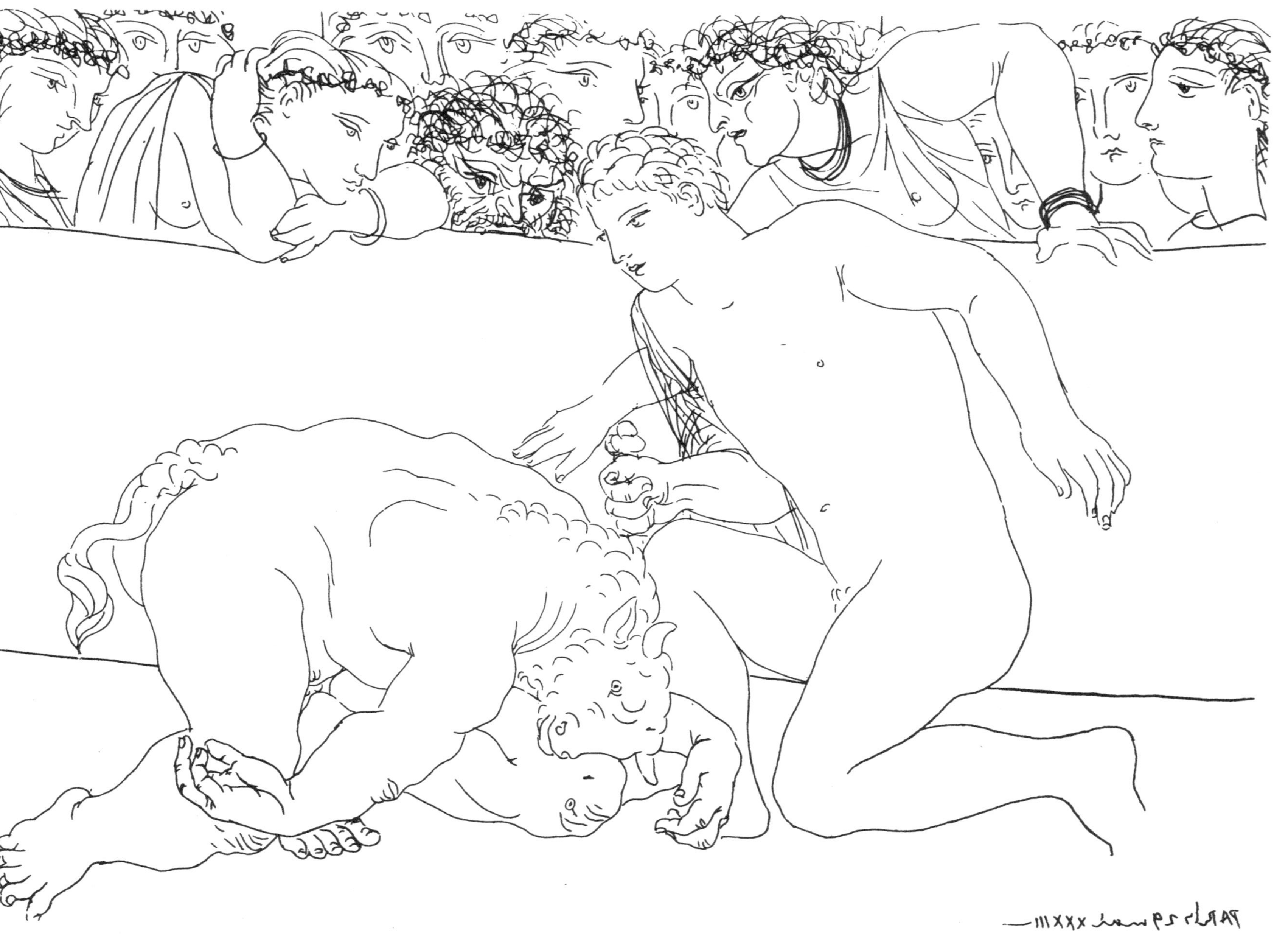

Minotaur in the Arena, Conquered by a Young Man. 1933. Etching. 19.3 x 26.9 cm (7⅝ x 10⅝ inches).

Dying Minotaur in the Arena. 1933. Etching. 19.3 x 26.8 cm (7¾ x 10⁹⁄₁₆ inches).

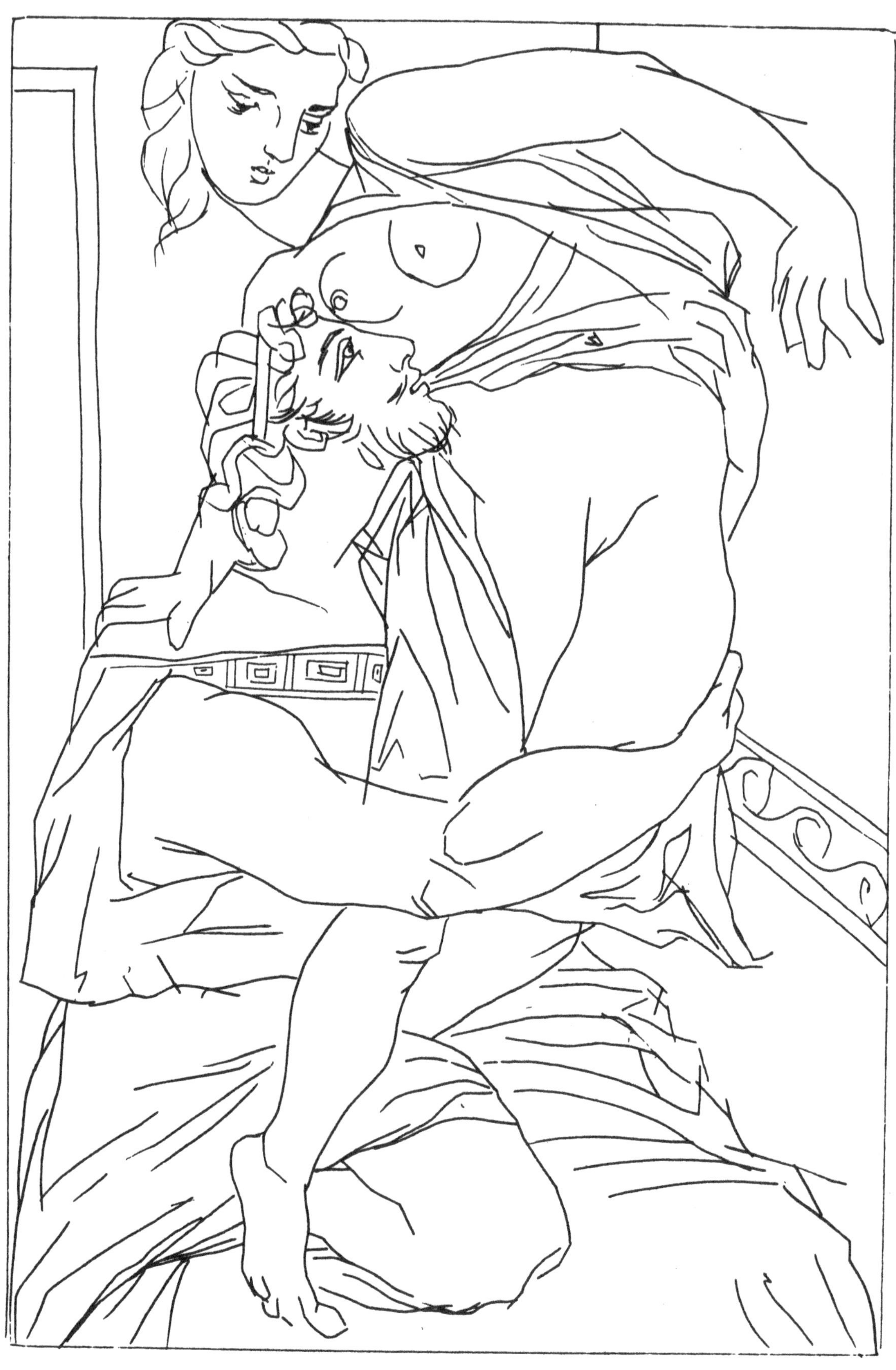

 ILLUSTRATION FROM "LYSISTRATA." 1934. Etching. 21.1 x 13.9 cm (8⁵⁄₁₆ x 5½ inches).

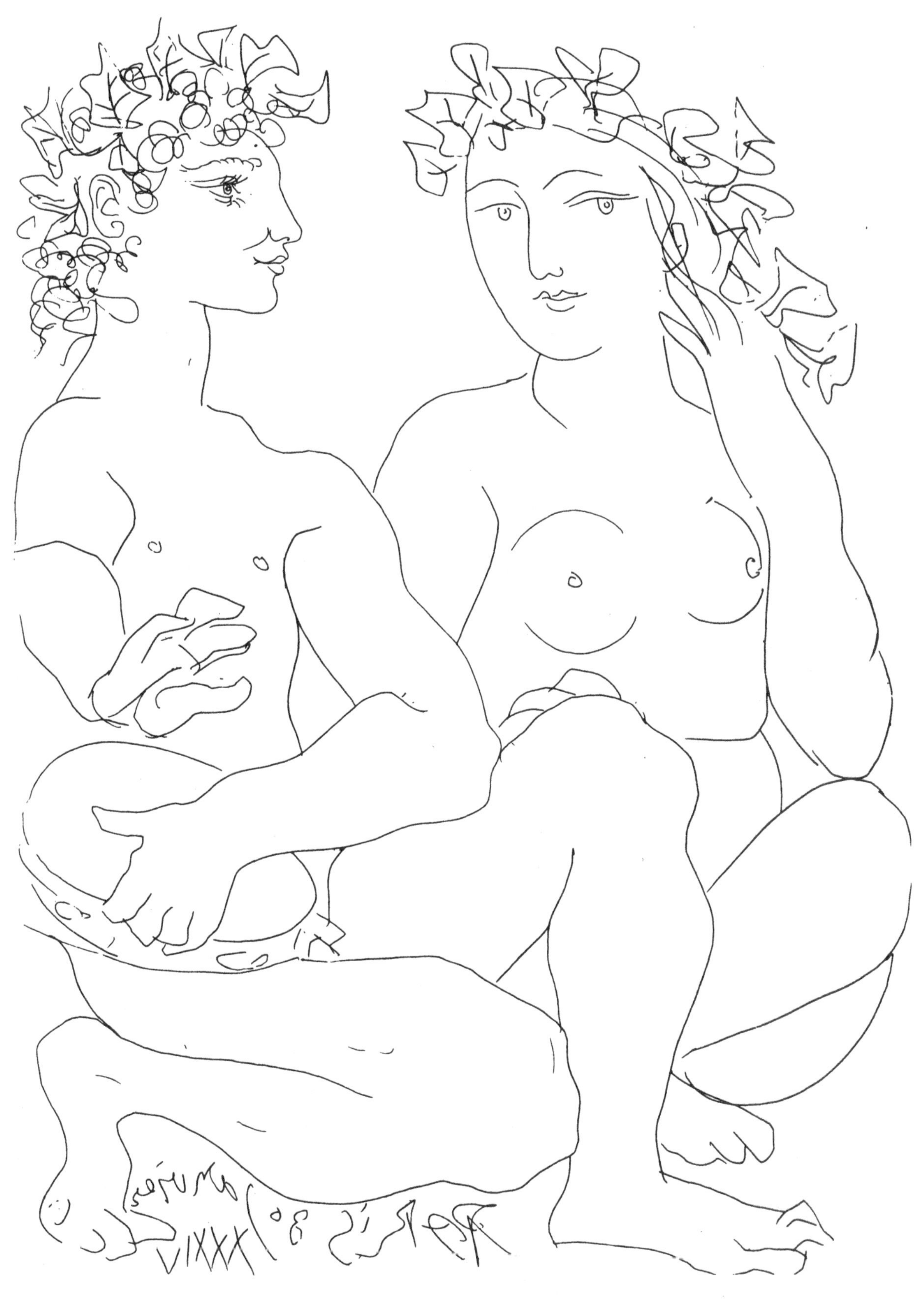

NUDE WITH TAMBOURINE PLAYER. 1934. Etching. 27.7 x 19.7 cm ($10^{15}/_{16}$ x $7^{13}/_{16}$ inches).

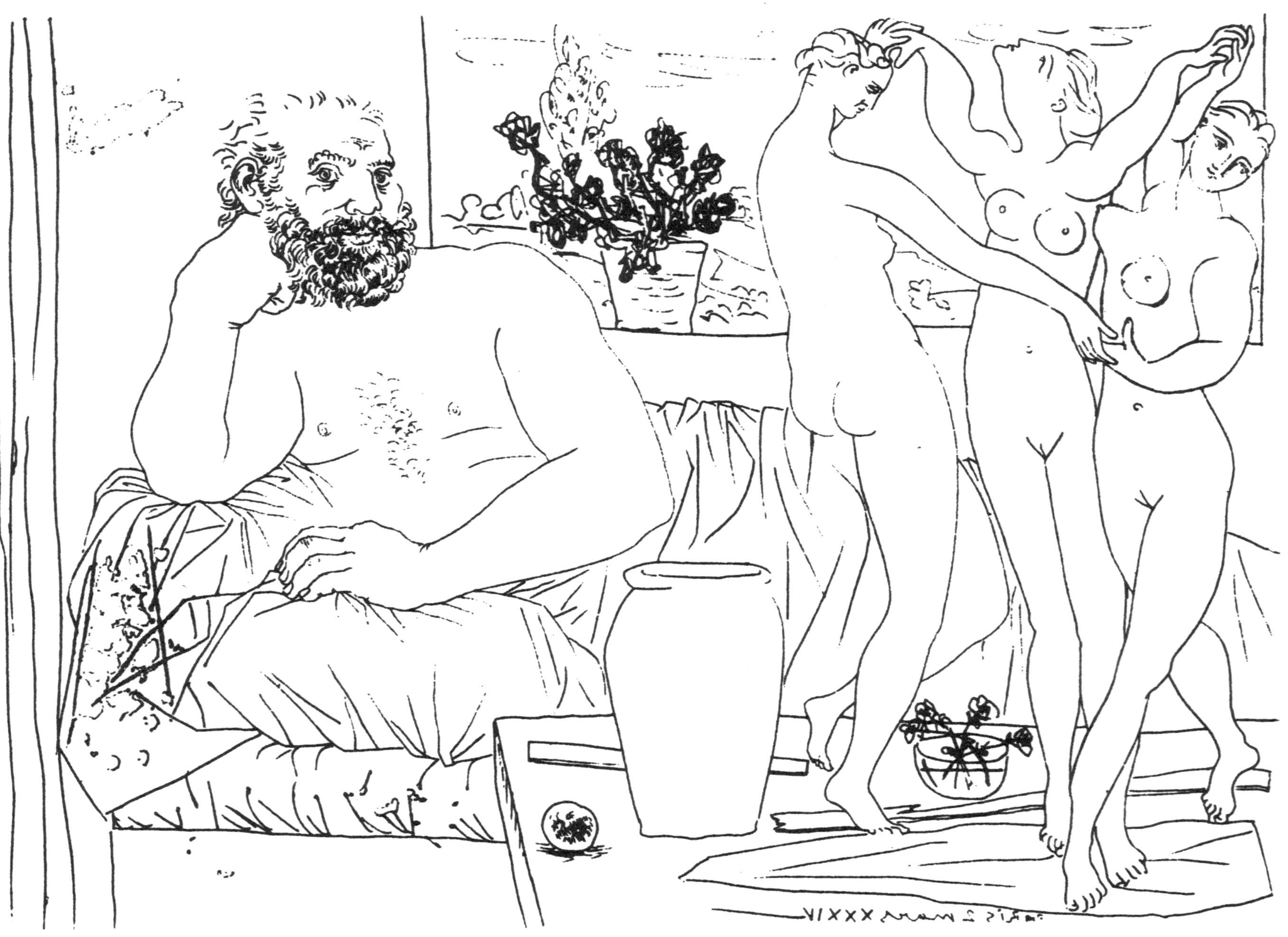

Sculptor and Three Dancers. 1934. Combined technique. 22.3 x 31.3 cm (8⅞ x 12¹⁵⁄₁₆ inches).

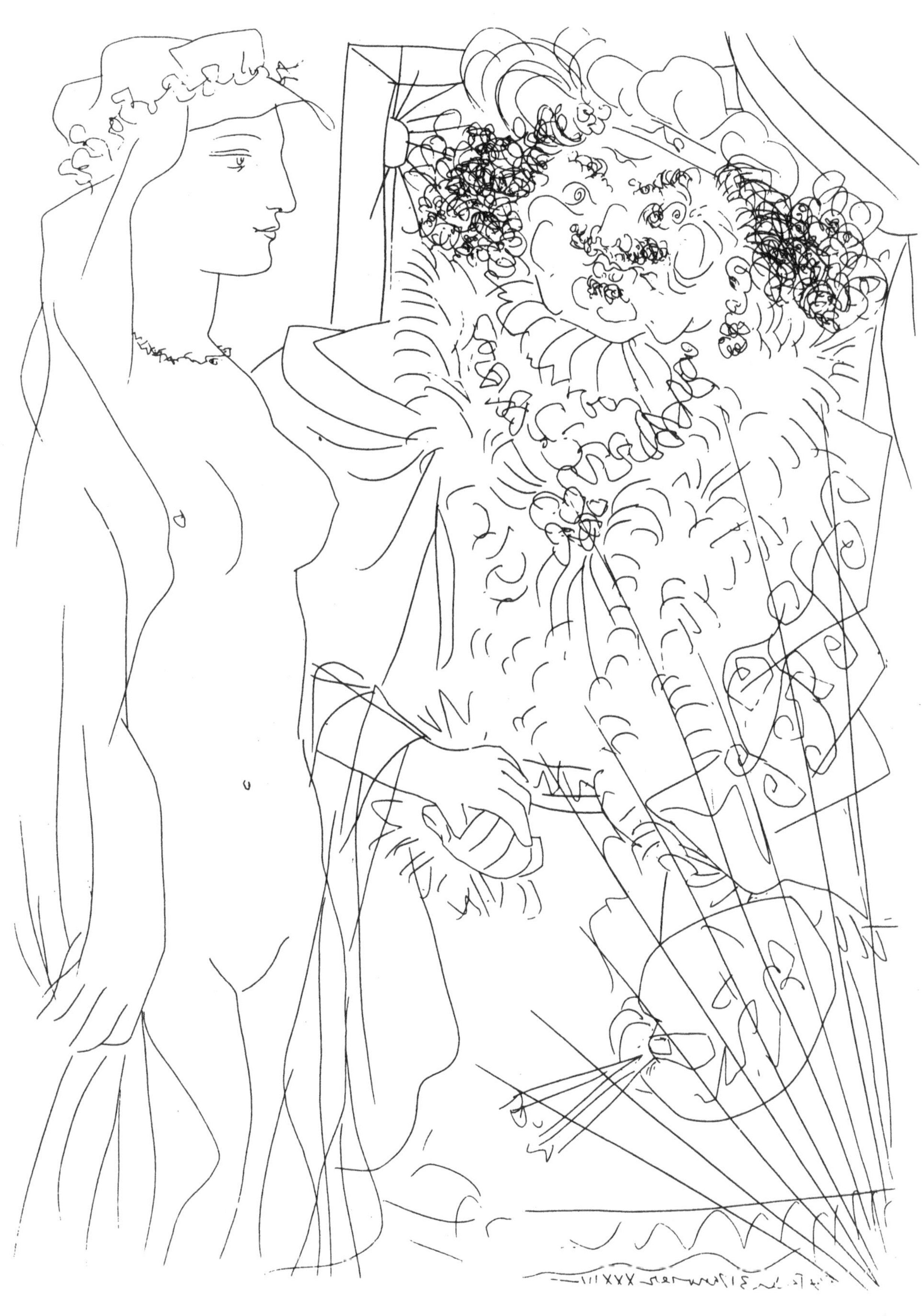

Semidraped Model Standing Before Rembrandt, Who Holds a Palette. 1934.
Etching. 27.8 x 19.8 cm (10^{15}⁄$_{16}$ x 7^{13}⁄$_{16}$ inches).

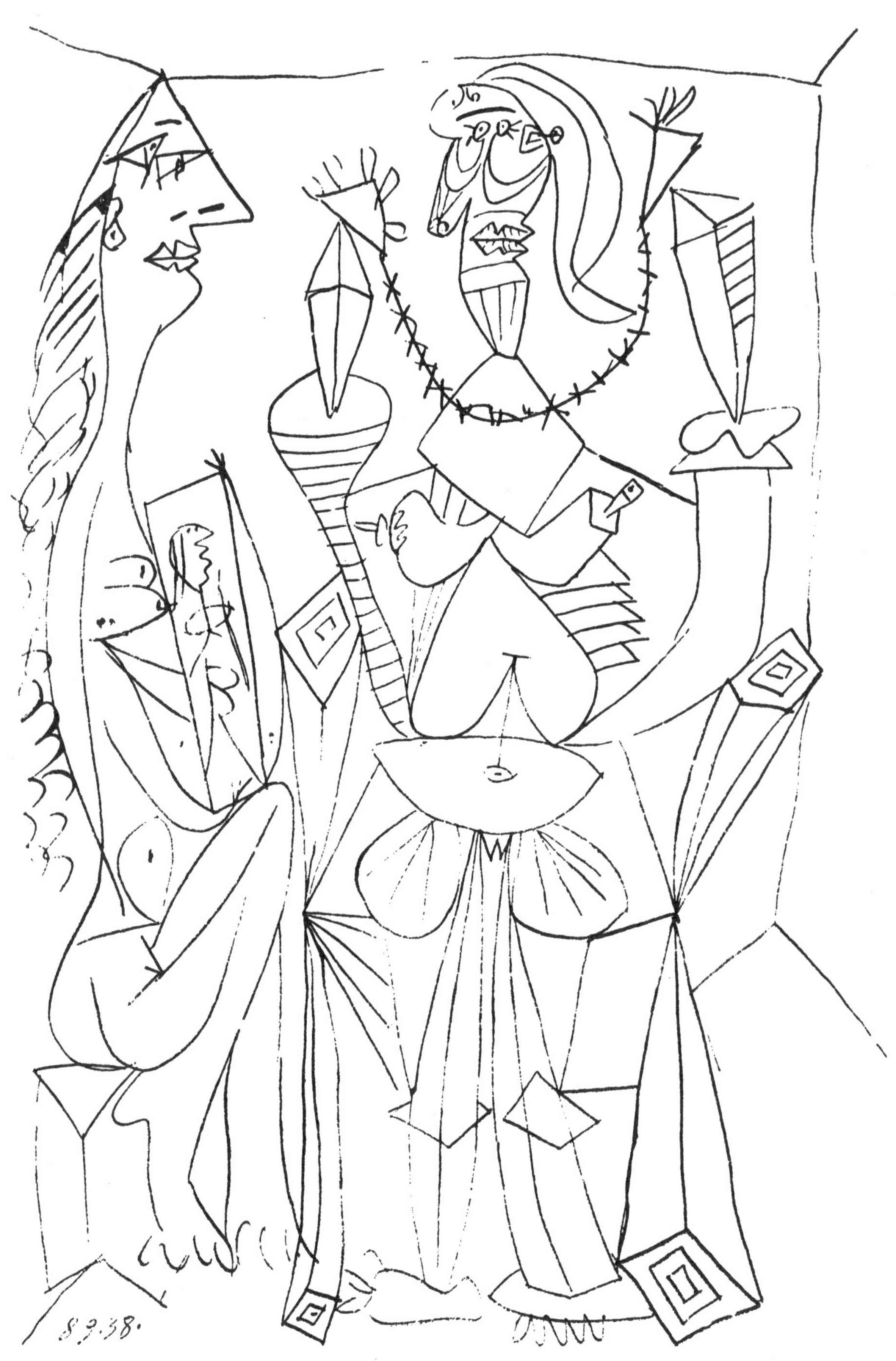

Two Seated Women. 1938. Drawing in India ink. 67.5 x 53 cm (26^{15}/$_{16}$ x 20^{7}/$_8$ inches).

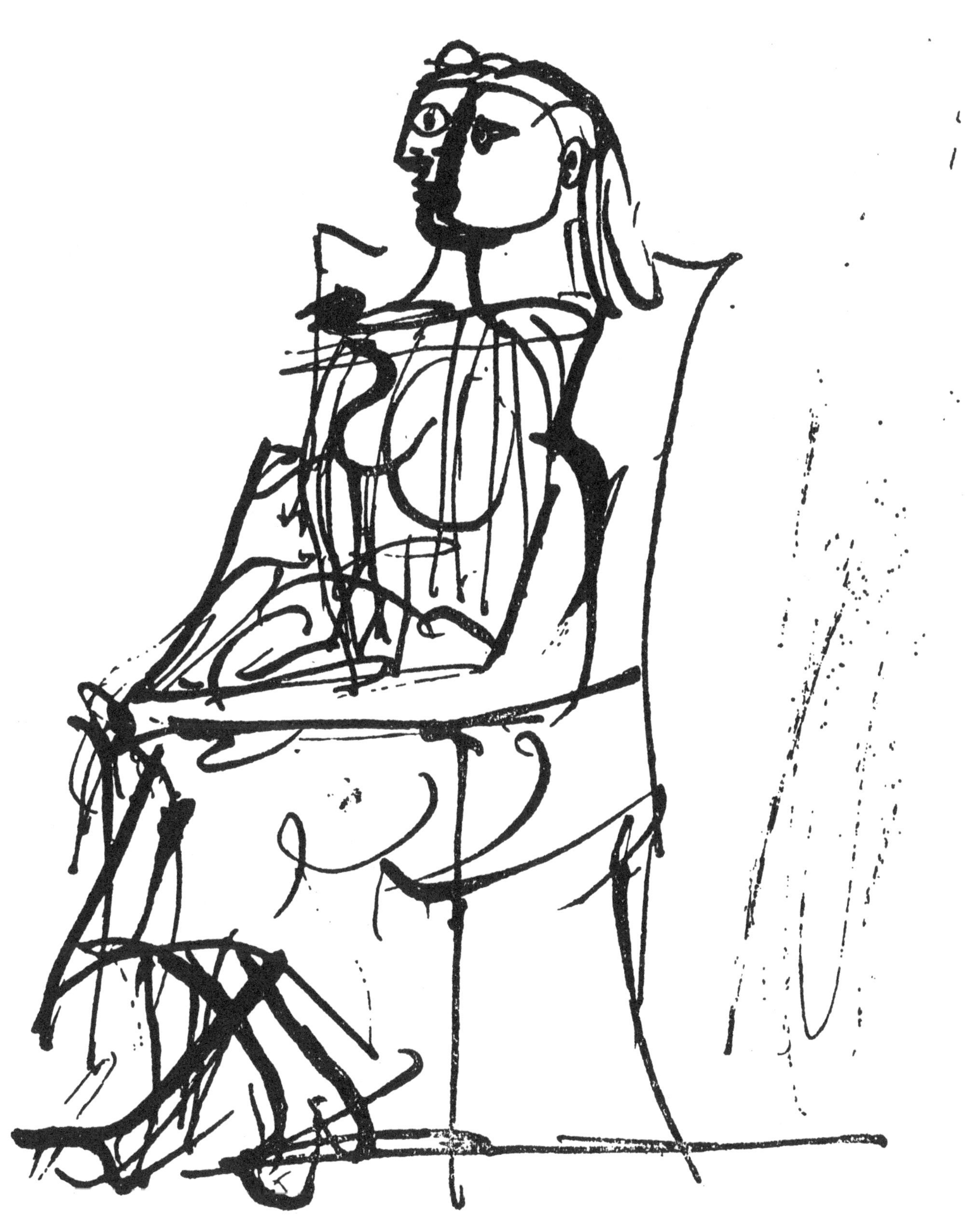

STUDY. 1938. Drawing in India ink. One of two on a page. 45 x 24 cm (17¾ x 9⁷⁄₁₆ inches).

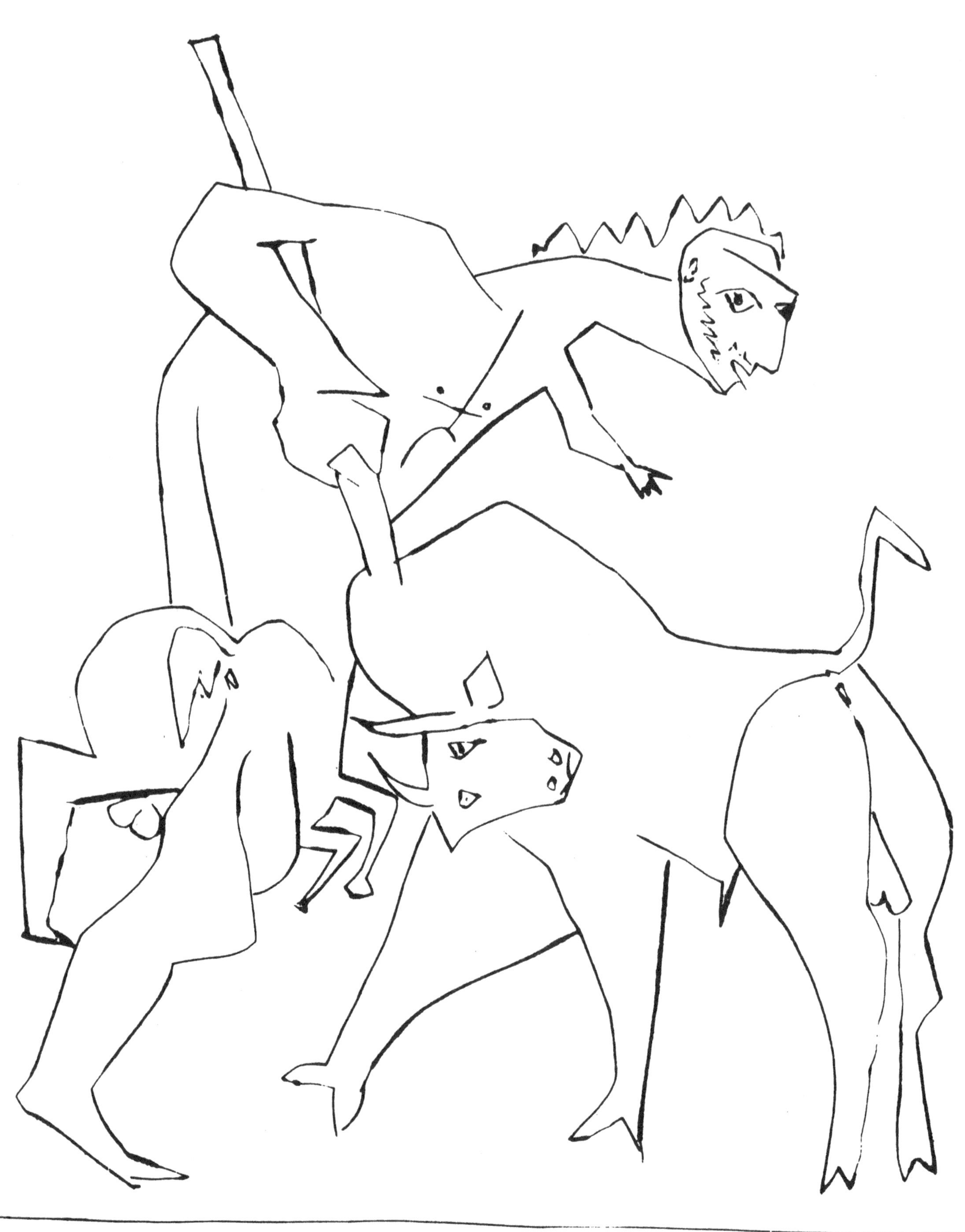

ILLUSTRATION FOR RAMON REVENTOS' "DEUX CONTES." 1947. Etching.

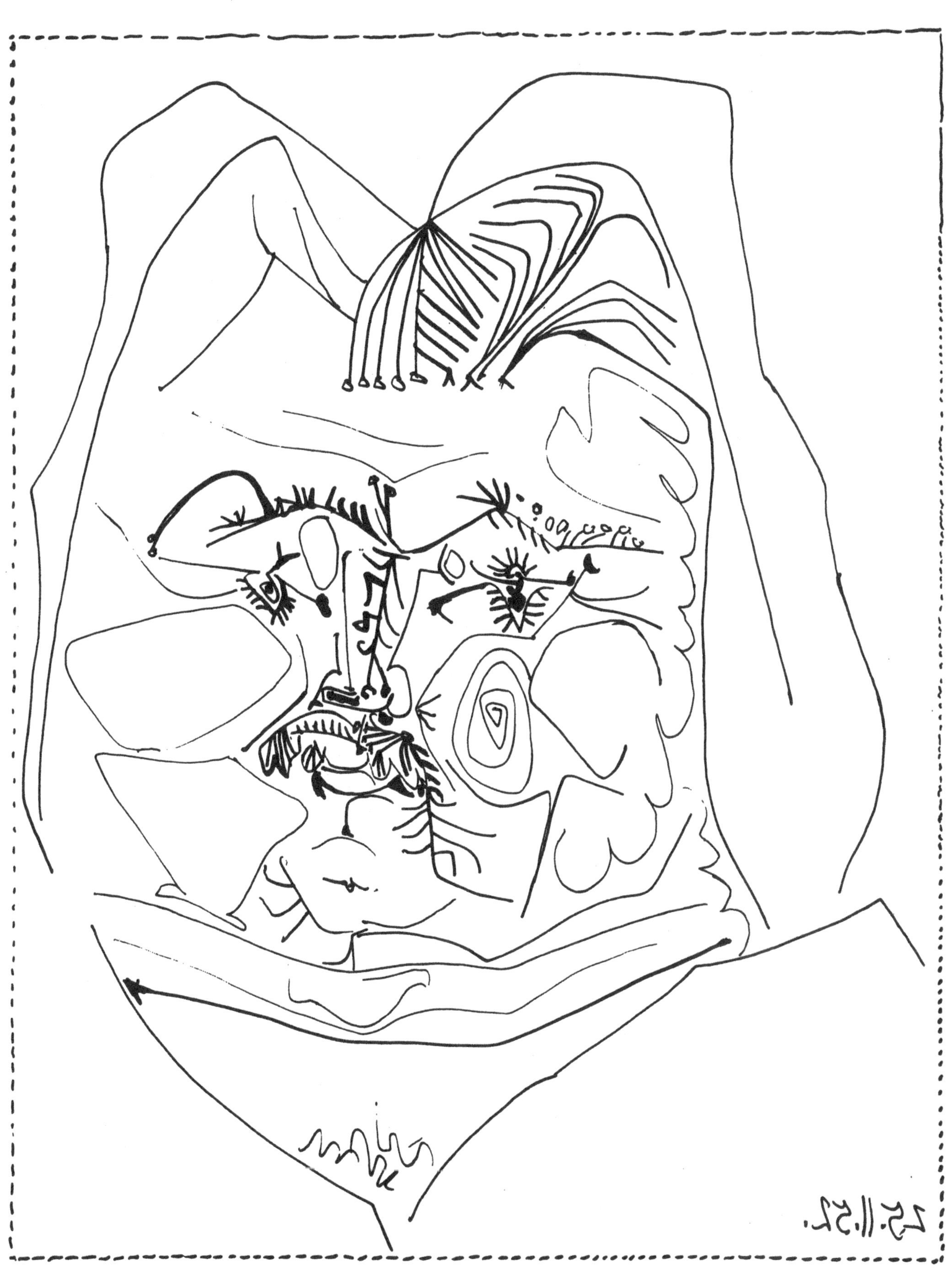

Balzac. 1952. Lithograph. 70 x 53.2 cm (27^{15}/$_{16}$ x 20^{15}/$_{16}$ inches).

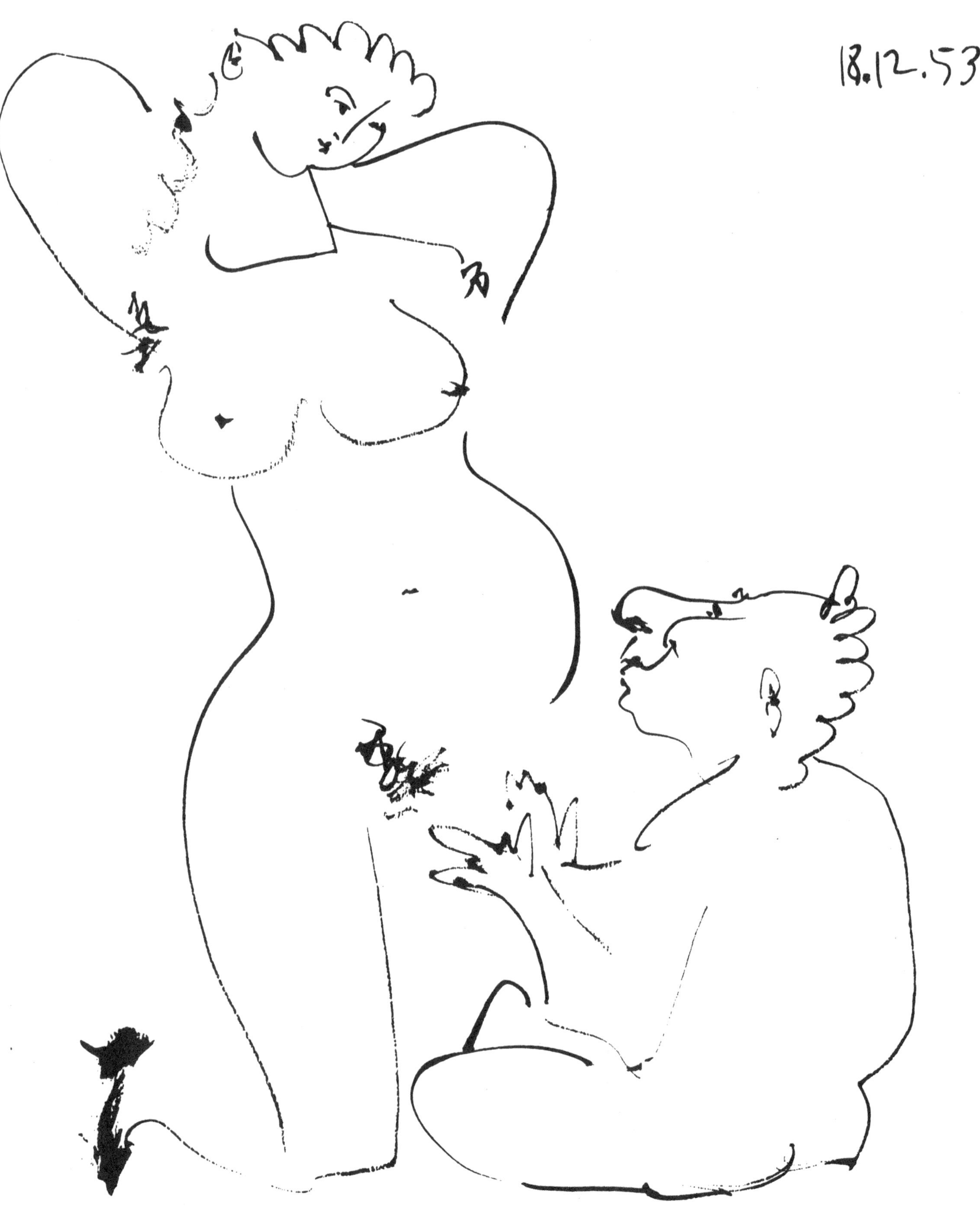

WOMAN AND DWARF. 1953. Drawing in India ink. 35 x 26.5 cm (13¾ x 10⁷⁄₁₆ inches).

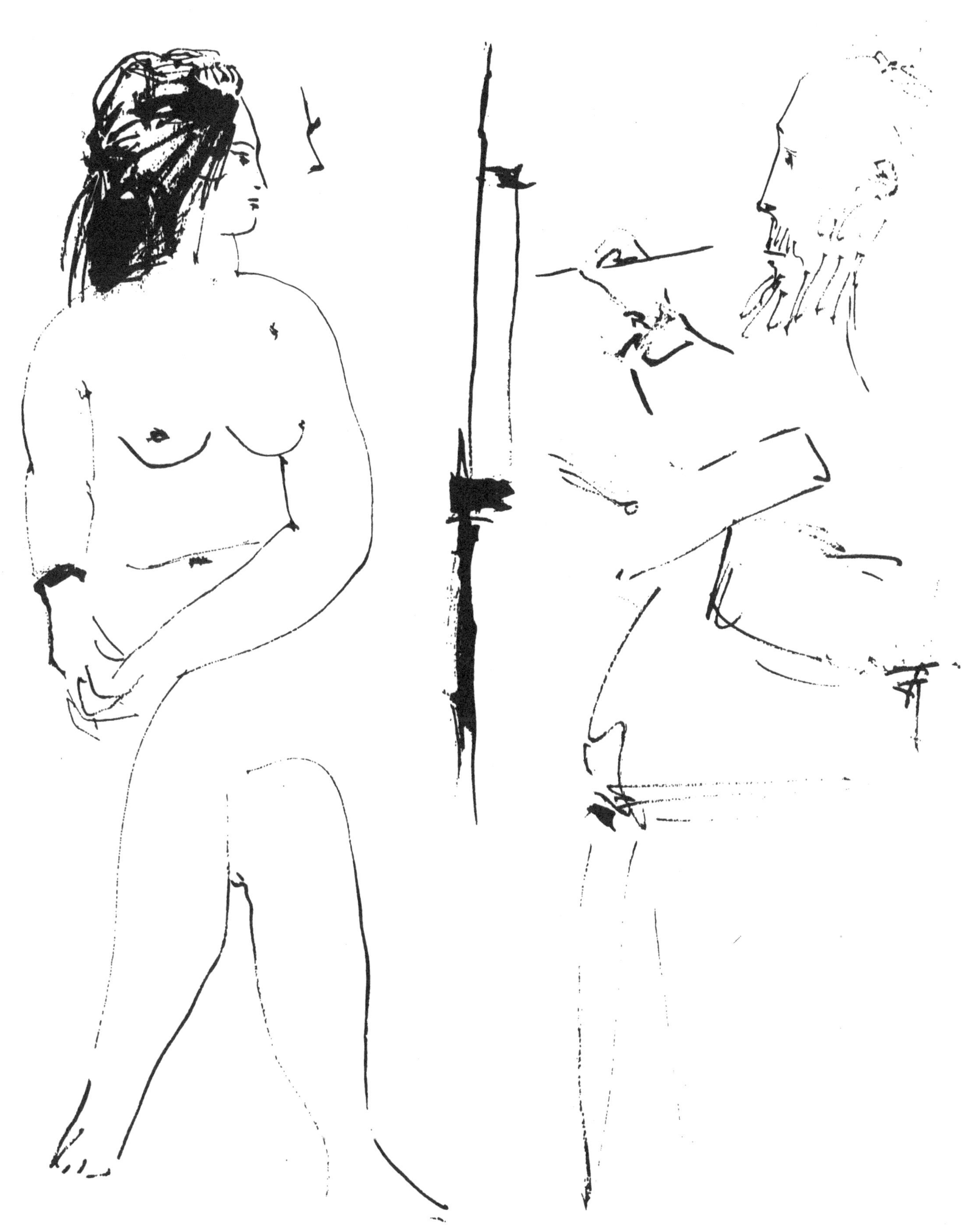

Painter and Model. 1953. Drawing in India ink. 35 x 26.5 cm (13¾ x 10⁷⁄₁₆ inches).

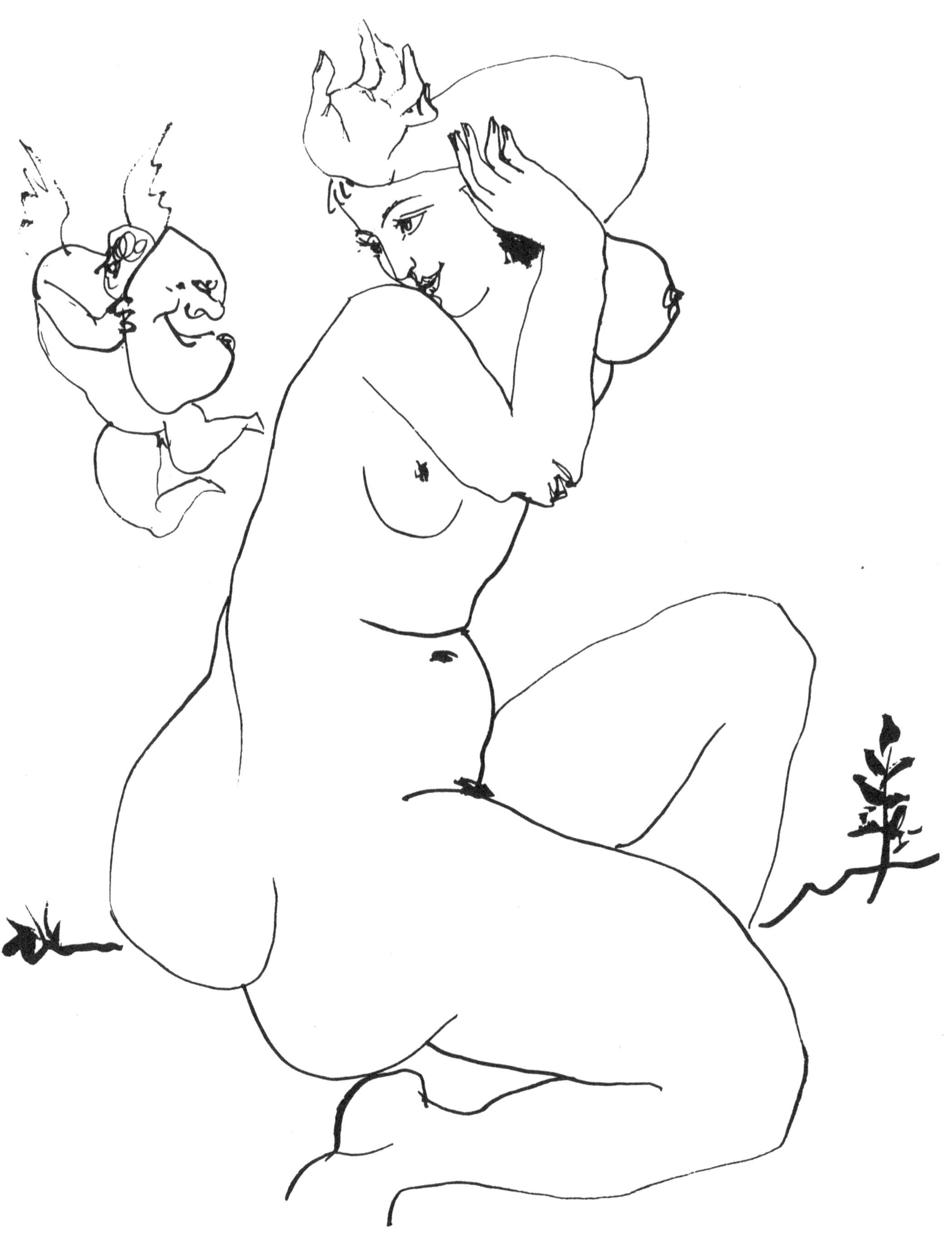

 WOMAN AND CUPID. 1954. Drawing in India ink. 32 x 24 cm (12⅝ x 9⁷⁄₁₆ inches).

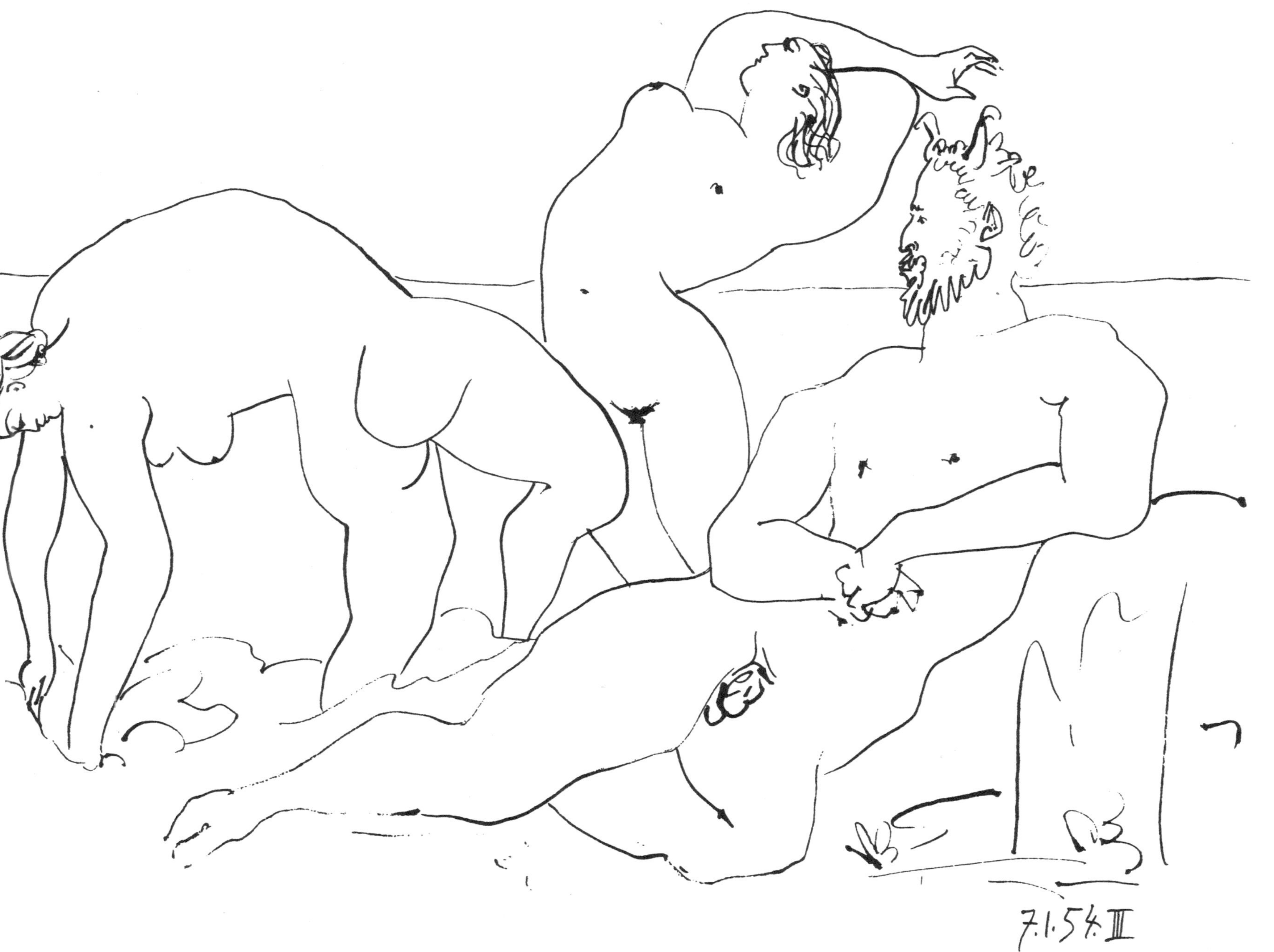

At the Seashore. 1954. Drawing in India ink. 24 x 32 cm ($9\frac{7}{16}$ x $12\frac{5}{8}$ inches).

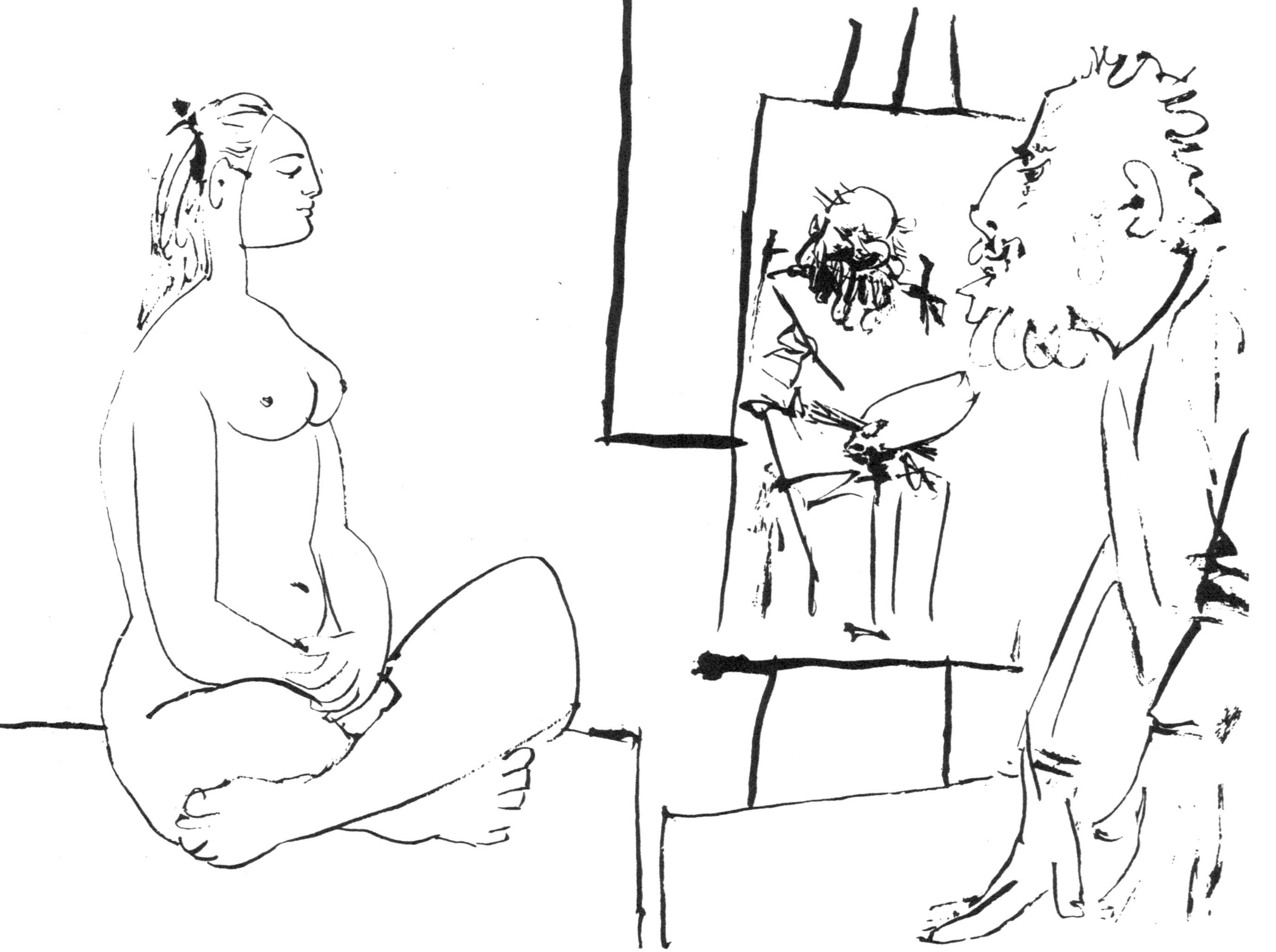

THE MASKED MODEL. 1954. Wash drawing. 24 x 32 cm (9⁷⁄₁₆ x 12⁵⁄₈ inches).

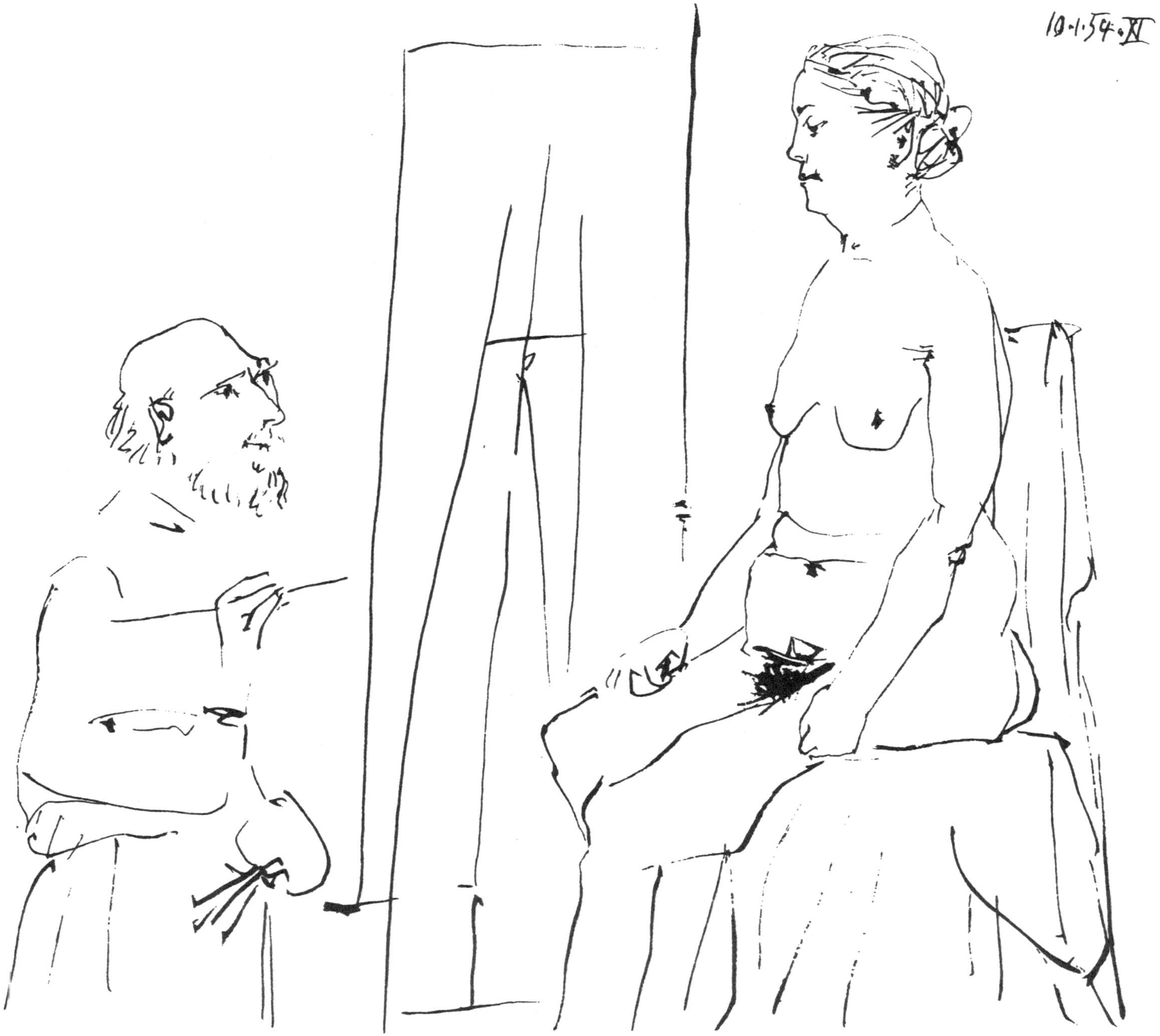

THE OLD MODEL. Drawing in India ink. 24 x 32 cm ($9\frac{7}{16}$ x $12\frac{5}{8}$ inches).